Brexit and the Car Industry

One of the principal arguments put forth by Brexit supporters is that by freeing the UK from the stranglehold of EU law, the country will be able to expand its markets through increased bilateral trade and enhance economic growth. This book tests this proposition by reference to the car industry.

Brexit and the Car Industry explores the international position of the car market to argue that the hope of Brexit bringing regulatory freedom is illusory. The book starts by examining the structure of the vehicle industry, how its regulatory framework evolved and how the environment in which it operates is constrained by international standards and the practicalities associated with trading across different regulatory systems. By examining the evolution of vehicle regulations, particularly related to the environment, it argues that a UK independent path is not only impractical but also self-defeating. The private car market is structured in such a way that is global, and meeting the various international regulatory requirements is a price of entry requirement which no bilateral trade agreements are likely to alter. The book also considers the changing environment affecting the car industry in the context of an aspiration for regulatory freedom. The response to climate change and the impact of technological change – specifically driverless vehicles – are big questions for the industry and both are examined in this book. The book also considers the emergence of large metropolitan areas imposing their own use and environmental requirements operating separately to national standards. The future of electric and autonomous vehicles combined with the complexity of the regulatory environment with both international and localised pollution measures make the UK navigating a safe independent path through with a viable car industry highly questionable.

Providing a comprehensive review of the relationship between regulatory frameworks and free trading models, this book is aimed at industry and legal professionals. It will also be of interest to students studying market behaviour, free trade law and the free movement of goods and environmental protection.

Matthew Humphreys MBE is Professor of Law, Dean and Head of School at Royal Holloway, University of London and Professor at the University of Notre Dame, London.

Douglas Munro is a Business Economist with academic experience in the US, UK and Kuwait and a former automotive executive who worked for more than three decades in North America, South America, Europe, the Middle East and Africa.

Legal Perspectives on Brexit

Series Editor: Richard Lang, University of Brighton, UK
Editorial Board: David Edward CMG, QC, MA, LLB, LLD, FRSE
(University of Edinburgh, UK, Emeritus)
Margot Horspool (University of Surrey, UK, Emeritus)
Shirley McDonagh (CILEx, UK)

'Legal Perspectives on Brexit' is a peer-reviewed series of shortform books which goes beyond responding to public curiosity aroused by the triggering of Article 50 to recognize the ongoing legal and political disputes Brexit has prompted. Aimed at academics and professionals it provides expert commentary on and predictions about the possible legislative and judicial implications of Brexit for each of the different sectors of regulation which have for so long been dominated by EU Law, creating a valuable one stop resource which exposes, explores and perhaps even resolves legal problems stemming from the separation of UK and EU legal systems.

Brexit and Aviation Law
Jan Walulik

Brexit and Procurement Law
Catherine Maddox

Brexit and the Car Industry
Matthew Humphreys and Douglas Munro

Forthcoming

Brexit and Intellectual Property Law
Janice Denoncourt

Brexit and Competition Law
Andreas Stephan and Barry Rodger

Brexit and Energy Law
Raphael Heffron

https://www.routledge.com/law/series/BREXIT

Brexit and the Car Industry

**Matthew Humphreys
and Douglas Munro**

LONDON AND NEW YORK

First published 2019
by Routledge
2 Park Square, Milton Park, Abingdon, Oxon OX14 4RN

and by Routledge
52 Vanderbilt Avenue, New York, NY 10017

Routledge is an imprint of the Taylor & Francis Group, an informa business

© 2019 Matthew Humphreys and Douglas Munro

The right of Matthew Humphreys and Douglas Munro to be identified as authors of this work has been asserted by them in accordance with sections 77 and 78 of the Copyright, Designs and Patents Act 1988.

All rights reserved. No part of this book may be reprinted or reproduced or utilised in any form or by any electronic, mechanical, or other means, now known or hereafter invented, including photocopying and recording, or in any information storage or retrieval system, without permission in writing from the publishers.

Trademark notice: Product or corporate names may be trademarks or registered trademarks, and are used only for identification and explanation without intent to infringe.

British Library Cataloguing-in-Publication Data
A catalogue record for this book is available from the British Library

Library of Congress Cataloging-in-Publication Data
Names: Humphreys, Matthew James, 1969– author. |
Munro, Douglas, 1949 January 21– author.
Title: Brexit and the car industry / Matthew Humphreys and Doug Munro.
Description: 1 Edition. | New York: Routledge, 2019. |
Series: Legal perspectives on Brexit |
Identifiers: LCCN 2019011124 (print) | LCCN 2019017007 (ebook) |
ISBN 9780429023873 (ebk) | ISBN 9780367086985 (hbk)
Subjects: LCSH: European Union—Great Britain. |
Great Britain—Politics and government—2007– |
Automobile industry and trade—Law and legislation—
Great Britain. | Automobile industry and trade—
Law and legislation—European Union countries.
Classification: LCC HC240.25.G7 (ebook) |
LCC HC240.25.G7 H86 2019 (print) |
DDC 338.4/7629222094—dc23
LC record available at https://lccn.loc.gov/2019011124

ISBN: 978-0-367-08698-5 (hbk)
ISBN: 978-0-429-02387-3 (ebk)

Typeset in Times New Roman
by codeMantra

Matthew
For Ian, my parents and all of my wonderfully supportive family.

Doug
For Tina, who somehow manages to put up with me and Harry Miller, who helps me think more clearly.

Contents

Preface	ix
Acknowledgements	xi
Abbreviations	xii
Table of legislation	xv

1	Introduction	1
2	Draft Brexit agreement proposals	6
3	Overview of the UK vehicle industry and its global position	11
4	EU market regulation affecting motor vehicles: product standards and rules of origin	30
5	International standards	44
6	Vehicle emissions impact	62
7	Regulation and the market	84
8	Disruptors	99
9	The role of cities	118

viii *Contents*

10 What if it gets ugly?   127

11 Final thoughts   134

Appendix I: dashboard   141
Index   145

Preface

In the run up to the referendum on UK membership of the EU, Matthew was invited to speak about the remain and leave positions at a Dagenham Chamber of Commerce debate. Other speakers at the debate included a representative from the CBI – the Confederation of British Industry, an economist and a member of the UKIP political party. Dagenham has been the UK home to Ford motor cars since the 1930s and many questions from the floor concerned the potential impact of Brexit on the UK car industry. At the end of the debate, in a quick poll in the room, the audience by a show of hands were two-thirds in favour of staying in the EU. Dagenham – or more precisely, residents of Barking and Dagenham as a borough – however voted for leave by 62.4% to 37.6% for remain. Ford's European boss, Steven Armstrong, in raising concerns about the prospects for the UK car industry if the UK leaves the EU without a deal in October 2018, queried the continuing viability of Ford in the UK without 'frictionless' access to the EU market.

Brexit proponents believe the UK, unencumbered from EU shackles, will expand its markets, and for the motor industry, there are suggestions that the UK could join the US, Canada and Mexico trade pact. However, the interest of the US vehicle industry in the UK has been almost non-existent. The 'bible' of Detroit's vehicle manufacturers, the weekly *Automotive News*, had only 19 mentions of Brexit between 2017 and the end of 2018, mostly related to the impact of the fall of the pound. In fact, the sole article on the potential to join the North American trade agreement referred to it as a "nonstarter" (Gibbs, 2017, p. 32). As further evidence of the US auto industry position, the remaining US automaker in Europe, Ford, announced a major European restructuring in January 2019 that is expected to lead to thousands of job losses including in the UK. While no specific cuts were announced at that time, and Ford European boss Steven Armstrong insisted that

x   *Preface*

"This is not a consequence of the Brexit situation", he added that "If Brexit goes in the wrong direction…we would need to look again about what we could do to mitigate the impact of that (BBC, 2018)". Expectation that the North American vehicle market awaiting a newly liberated UK is wishful thinking.

Much has and will still be said about Brexit. This book is intended as a contribution to the discussions focussing on a specific area of industry – an industry that both reflects important national concerns about identity and economy, an industry facing great change as technological development rapidly supersedes previous norms and an industry which is much the focus of international political attention from the perspective of sustainable development and the threat of climate change. The book is intended as an introduction to the bigger debate about Brexit for those unfamiliar with it while focussing on a specific area of Brexit impact for those all too familiar with the debate. The book seeks to work both in legal and business academic contexts. It is becoming practically impossible for the business and the legal contexts to be kept separate in the Brexit debate and in fact the intertwining of both is, we hope, a better way forward. This book hopes to serve as a guide and as a basis for further studies of the subject. Please note that due to the timeliness of Brexit as a subject, many of the references in this book are current publications. Some of those publications may be available by subscription only, but which may be accessible at libraries.

References

BBC. (2018). *Porsche stops making diesel cars after VW emissions scandal.* 23 September. Retrieved from https://www.bbc.com/news/world-europe-45619994

Gibbs, N. (2017). UK joining NAFTA? Intriguing, but unlikely. *Automotive News.*

Acknowledgements

We would like to thank Alexander Brown for the various contributions made to this project and Alison Kirk for giving us the impetus. We also appreciate the responsive and helpful staff at the Office for National Statistics who directed us towards appropriate data sets.

Detroit and London
February 2019

Abbreviations

Throughout this book, a number of abbreviations are used to save space and to make the text more concise:

ABI	Association of British Insurers
ABS	Antilock braking system
ACEA	European Automobile Manufacturers Association
AC	Alternating current
AECC	Association for Emissions Control by Catalyst
APA	American Psychological Association
AV	Autonomous vehicle
BEIS	Department for Business, Energy & Industrial Strategy
CAFE	Corporate Average Fuel Economy (US)
CARS 2020	EU high level group for auto industry competitiveness
CHMSL	Centred High Mounted Stop Light
CJEU	Court of Justice of the European Union
CI	Consumers International
CKD	Completely knocked down
CO_2	Carbon dioxide
DC	Direct current
DARPA	Defense Advanced Research Program Agency
E01295	Working Group on Motor Vehicles
EC	European Community
ECOSOC	United Nations Economic and Social Committee
EEA	European Economic Area
EEC	European Economic Community
EPA	Environmental Agency (US)
ESC	Electronic Stability Control
ETRTO	European Tyre and Rim Technical Organisation
EU	European Union

Euro 1–6	System of EU emission standards
EUROMOT	European Association of Internal Combustion Manufacturers
EV	Electric vehicle
FCA	Facilitated Customs Arrangement
FMVSS	Federal Motor Vehicle Safety Standards
FTA	Free Trade Agreement
GDP	Gross Domestic Product
GEAR 2030	EU high level group for industry competitiveness and sustainable growth
GHG	Greenhouse gas
GPU	Graphic Processing Unit
GRPE	Groupes des Reportuers
GTR	Global Technical Regulations (under the UN 1998 Agreement)
HAV	Highly Automated Vehicle
ISOFIX	International Standard for Attaching Child Safety Seats
IMF	International Monetary Fund
LED	Light emitting diode
MFN	Most Favoured Nation
NEDC	New European Driving Cycle
NEHIS	National Institute of Environmental Health Sciences (US)
NHTSA	National Highway Traffic Safety Agency (US)
NH_3	Ammonia
NMVOC	Non-methane volatile organic compound
NOx	Nitrogen oxide
NYPD	New York Police Department
OEM	Original Equipment Manufacturer
OICA	Organisation of Motor Vehicle Manufacturers
OJ	Official Journal of the European Communities
ONS	Office for National Statistics
OPEC	Organisation of Petroleum Exporting Countries
PEMS	Portable Emission Measuring System
$PM_{2.5}$	Particulate matter
RDE	Real Driving Emission Test
RVIA	Recreation Vehicle Industry Association
SAE	Society of Automotive Engineers
SEA	Single European Act
SMMT	Society of Motor Manufacturers and Traders
SO_2	Sulphur dioxide

xiv *Abbreviations*

TFEU	Treaty on the Functioning of the European Union
TPS	Toyota Production System
ULEZ	Ultra Low Emission Zone
UN	United Nations
UNECE	United Nations Economic Commission for Europe
UNGTR	United Nations Global Technical Regulation (under 1998 Agreement)
WBIA	World Bicycle Industry Association
WHO	World Health Organisation
WP.29	World Forum for Harmonisation of Vehicle Regulations
WLTP	World-Harmonised Light-duty Vehicle Test Procedure
WTO	World Trade Organization
WVTA	Whole Vehicle Type-Approval System

Table of legislation

European Union acts

Directive 70/220/EEC on motor vehicle air pollution OJ L 76, 6.4.1970, pp. 1–22

Directive 92/53/EEC on the type-approval of motor vehicles OJ L 225, 10.8.1992, pp. 1–62

Directive 2007/46/EC on a framework for vehicle approval OJ L 263, 9.10.2007, pp. 1–160

Regulation 443/2009/EU setting emission performance standards for new passenger cars OJ L 140, 5.6.2009, pp. 1–15

Regulation 2016/679/EU on the processing of personal data OJ L 119, 4.5.2016, pp. 1–88

Regulation 2018/858/EU on approval and market surveillance of motor vehicles etc OJ L 151, 14.6.2018, pp. 1–218

European Economic Area Agreement

UK legislation

European Union (Notification of Withdrawal) Act 2017

Road Traffic Act 1988

Treaty provisions

Treaty on European Union, article 50

Treaty on the functioning of the European Union, articles 10, 28, 30, 34 and 35

Other acts

Vienna Convention on the Law of Treaties 1969

Australian Personal Property Security Act 2009

Californian Vehicle Code

1 Introduction

Industry and nations, or national identities, have a range of associations but it is clear that for some industries the association of brand and nation is close. Perhaps the classic example is the national airline which typifies an industry, even if these carriers struggle with low-cost hauliers in an intensively competitive environment. The airline business is still populated by players including Air France, British Airways, Finnair and Austrian Airways (now in reality a subsidiary of the German Lufthansa). Raguraman noted how the separation of Singapore from the federation of Malaysia inexorably led to the splitting of Malaysian and Singapore Airways into two new national carriers, with different underpinning objectives reflecting the different political priorities of the new states (Raguraman, 1997). Each new state felt it was important to have a national airline. For the car industry, the branding of Jaguar, Mercedes-Benz, Citroen, Fiat and perhaps slightly differently, Lada and Trabant as national icons is difficult to disentangle from assessments of quality or real differences between the products. There was something particularly 'British' both in aspiration and in markers of quality about Jaguar products, whereas the Trabant has about as many advocates today as its long defunct DDR – East German – home.

The campaign to separate the UK from the EU and/or the European market, which culminated in the referendum in 2016 and the subsequent decisions to leave, had many drivers but there was an underpinning aspiration for the rebirth of national industries. As the progress with the leavers' dream fulfilment has proven more tortuous than expected, or suggested at the time of the campaign, the sense of missed opportunity is perhaps one thing that genuinely unites those in both leave and remain camps.

While the campaign to leave the EU was not necessarily much to do with the car industry, it is also entirely to do with it. The motor industry experience of Brexit well expresses both the complex arguments

2 Introduction

for national identity and the expectation that separateness is needed to express that identity. It also addresses the complex question of what defines a British industry in a global market with all its supply chain dynamics. Perhaps most clearly unresolved throughout this protracted debate is the question of how an industry can flourish and is expressed as well by the motor industry in the time of Brexit as any other industry. How the UK car industry will fare with Brexit is the focus of this book.

At this point in time, it is perilous to forecast the outcome of Brexit; there are simply too many unknowns. The European Union (Notification of Withdrawal) Act 2017 triggered notification under the EU treaties for the UK to leave the EU on 29 March 2019. This has subsequently, by agreement with the European Council, been extended twice and the new envisaged day for the UK's departure is 31 October 2019 although an earlier date is possible if the withdrawal agreement passes through the UK Parliament. At the same time, after two reschedules, further rescheduling is clearly possible. So there is a deadline but there are certain to be many twists and turns both before and after that date. Fortunately (or not) for the motor vehicle industry in the UK, many of the outcomes are likely to occur whether there is Brexit or not. Any plausible Brexit scenario will only exacerbate and accelerate those outcomes. The main reason for this is that the motor vehicle industry globally is entering, or perhaps already in, its greatest transition since the invention of the "horseless carriage". A combination of factors including battery innovations for electric cars and increasing enhancements to vehicle automation combined with greater concern for congestion and municipal environmental conditions are leading to much rethinking of the role of vehicles in society.

The debate around Brexit is happening at the same time as, but with remarkably little consideration of, intensified debate about climate change and environmental protection. The global threat of environmental degradation is generally accepted but there are maverick outliers who believe the threat is limited. There is widespread agreement that the response to climate change must be both international and coordinated, even if the specifics of what needs to be done to minimise environmental harm are difficult to agree (McGrath, 2018; UNFCCC, 2015). Depending then on the extent to which it is agreed that environmental threats are urgent, there is something quite jarring and inconsistent about both seeking international collaboration and national separation. It makes sense to back remaining in the EU and seeing the urgency of collective international responses to climate change, and it makes sense to reject both the need for the EU on Brexit terms and the

Introduction 3

need for international collaboration for environmental reasons. But a middle ground of supporting international collaboration at the same time as promoting an independent UK trade policy, or whatever other motivation for Brexit, seeking to promote national distinctiveness and the problems with such distinctiveness simultaneously appears problematic.

Environmental standards and their interface with trading rules present an interesting motor industry-related issue. In Chapter 6, we examine the varying environmental requirements that are imposed on vehicle manufacturers. The regulations in each market are fundamentally price of entry requirements. The requirements essentially fall into two groups – one set determined by the US and the second through the UN, although largely driven by the EU. Today the UK has a voice in those requirements through its membership in the EU. Post-Brexit, the UK will be required to follow whatever rules are determined by the larger players yet will have no role in shaping the outcome. This will become increasingly important as the rules evolve for electric vehicles. As a specific example, in 2020 the EU has stringent CO_2 targets coming into force. To assist manufacturers in their transition to electric vehicles a system of "super credits" will allow EU manufacturers to offset production of vehicles that fail to meet the targets. Unless something evolves in the Brexit negotiations that is not presently in place, UK vehicles will not count towards the targets, thus meaning that manufacturers will have an incentive to shift production out of the UK (Campbell, 2018).

States are not homogenous entities within which the motor industry can operate independently. Increasingly complex regulatory environments affect the manufacture and use of vehicles: the ability to drive a car of a certain product standard does not necessarily apply uniformly across a whole state with areas applying emissions standards or other licensing rules such as a congestion charge. Diesel vehicles are perfectly legal in all parts of the UK (at least as of today), but they cannot necessarily be parked everywhere, and manufacturers seek to adjust their product standards to meet both broad market standards and localised ones.

The invention of the electric vehicle preceded the internal combustion engine, and automated vehicles have been promised for the last half century with neither concept gaining major traction, but in the words of the late MIT economist Rudiger Dornbusch "...things take longer to happen than you think they will, and then they happen faster than you thought they could" (Summers, 2011). The vehicle industry may be at that tipping point. It just happens that this is transpiring as the Brexit process is unfolding.

4   *Introduction*

One of the principal arguments put forth by Brexit supporters is that by freeing the UK from the stranglehold of EU law, the country will be able to expand its markets through increased bilateral trade and enhance economic growth. This manuscript tests this proposition by reference to the vehicle industry. We examine the UK car market in its legal and global market context and argue that the promise of regulatory freedom may be real but will have little practical effect. To make the argument we:

- Summarise what the UK seems to want to achieve in Brexit;
- Survey the global vehicle industry and the UK's role in it;
- Examine the legal environment in which the vehicle industry operates;
- Address the ability of the UK vehicle industry to disentangle itself from the EU environmental regulatory framework;
- Review the relationship between regulatory frameworks and free trading models;
- Examine upcoming disruptors to the vehicle industry that will impact the UK regardless of Brexit;
- Explore the emergence of regulations such as congestion charges and air quality restrictions, operating at a localised or city-specific level that affect the use of cars independent of national controls; and
- Consider the possible outcome if Brexit proves to be a disaster for the UK car industry.

Through examining these issues we conclude that a UK independent path is not only impractical but self-defeating. We will review the composition of the global light vehicle market and demonstrate that meeting the various international regulatory requirements is indeed a price of entry requirement which bilateral trade agreements are unlikely to alter. We address the UK role in the global vehicle industry and argue that the role it plays in the economy pales in comparison to other industries that seem to be receiving less attention in the Brexit discussions. The book will also consider large metropolitan areas beginning to impose their own use and environmental requirements, which foreshadows the future of electric and autonomous vehicles, and is unlikely to benefit independent UK manufacturing. Finally, we take a look at what the impact on the UK economy would be if it were to lose its vehicle manufacturing base.

If, ultimately, the aspiration for a reinvigorated national car industry is unlikely to be delivered by Brexit, the industry's prospects can still be damaged by it. The argument is not just about Brexit but also considers the role of regulation in the car industry in a global market. The authors hope that this reference may prove to be of use to researchers in both legal and industry studies. Because of the limitless permutations of how Brexit may play out the specific outcomes may be modified and deferred, but the direction of the forces impacting change is almost certainly destined to occur.

References

Campbell. (2018). No-deal Brexit threatens electric car market. *Financial Times*. Retrieved from https://www.ft.com/content/c45cd3ae-b76a-11e8-bbc3-ccd7de085ffe

McGrath, M. (2018). *Katowice: COP24 Climate change deal to bring pact to life [Press release]*. Retrieved from https://www.bbc.com/news/science-environment-46582025

Raguraman, K. (1997). Airlines as instruments for nation building and national identity: case study of Malaysia and Singapore. *Journal of Transport Geography, 5*(4). Retrieved from https://www-sciencedirect-com.ezproxy01.rhul.ac.uk/science/article/pii/S0966692397000215.

Summers, L. (2011). The world must insist that Europe act. *Financial Times*. Retrieved from https://www.ft.com/content/5eaa83dc-dfca-11e0-b1db-00144feabdc0#axzz1YMpf3Yim

UNFCCC. (2015). *Paris Agreement*. United Nations. Retrieved from https://unfccc.int/files/essential_background/convention/application/pdf/english_paris_agreement.pdf

2 Draft Brexit agreement proposals

The UK government has interpreted the referendum result in 2016 as an instruction from the British people, to itself and to other state institutions, to organise the departure of the UK from the EU. It put through Parliament the European Union (Notification of Withdrawal) Act 2017, empowering the Prime Minister to start the departure process, and the government has treated the Brexit process as requiring first a formal withdrawal and subsequently agreements around future relationships between the UK and the EU. Previous expectations around being about to negotiate both the departure and the new relationship together and at the same time foundered (Carmona, Cîrlig, & Sgueo, 2018).

One of the challenges faced by the UK government in taking this interpretation of the referendum result has been that in seeking to fulfil this instruction from the people, the expectations about what is meant by departure and what future relationship between the UK and the EU is desired by the British people were not made clear in that referendum. The government sought to flesh out both its understanding of the popular will and its hopes for what can be realistically agreed in the July 2018 White Paper entitled *The future relationship between the United Kingdom and the European Union (UK Parliament, 2018)*.

This chapter considers the White Paper and sets out the principles that the UK government is seeking to apply in the withdrawal agreement and in negotiations as to the future relationship. The White Paper specifically refers to the motor vehicle industry although the reference is restricted to an acceptance of EU testing procedures for vehicles to ensure consistency of standards. We then consider the EU response to the White Paper and note the uncertain situation as to whether the future relationship will be as envisaged here. It is argued that the White Paper focus does not address the issues faced by the vehicle industry and further that the great uncertainty about the future relationship between the UK and the EU is itself an additional problem for the industry in the UK.

The White Paper

The White Paper posits that the UK wishes to develop two core partnerships: an economic partnership and a security partnership. These will stand alongside a hodgepodge of other collaborations referred to as "cross-cutting" cooperation that covers data, science, culture, education, defence, fishing and other items. The essence of the economic partnership is establishment by the UK and the EU of a free trade area for goods (UK Parliament, 2018, p. 13). This free trade area based on a phased implementation of a new Facilitated Customs Arrangement (FCA) is intended to provide "the most frictionless trade possible in goods between the UK and the EU" (UK Parliament, 2018, p. 16). This concept is accompanied by extensive suggestions for simplifying customs processes. It is clear that the UK government understands the risks of losing this particular freedom it enjoyed as part of the EU:

> Trade is essential for growth and prosperity. It stimulates greater business efficiency and higher productivity, sharing knowledge and innovation across the globe. Trade boosts jobs, raises living standards and provides a foundation for stronger and more prosperous communities. It ensures more people can access a wider choice of goods at lower cost, making household incomes go further.
>
> (UK Parliament, 2018, p. 47)

The government also seeks arrangement for services and digital that are not referred to as an FCA, although the language describing the concept closely mirrors the desired outcome for trade in goods. The proposal states that "The Government wants to minimise new barriers to trade between the UK and the EU" even as it recognises that there will be more barriers than is the case today (UK Parliament, 2018, p. 8). The difference appears to be that the government is seeking no tariffs on any goods, but "wants to chart its own path" when it comes to movement of services and data.

In tandem with the desired free movement of goods and services, the government also seeks the ability to move at least some people freely between the UK and the EU. There is recognition that integrated supply chains are at risk unless businesses are able to move personnel. Thus, the White Paper calls for the inclusion in trade agreements of provision to "seek reciprocal mobility arrangements with the EU...to support business to provide services and to move their talented people" (UK Parliament, 2018, pp. 32–33). There is also discussion about

8 *Draft Brexit agreement proposals*

the ability to allow students, scientists, sports people and individuals in cultural activities to move freely (UK Parliament, 2018, p. 83). The government appears to be walking a tight line between recognising that the free movement of people is as important as the free movement of goods yet respond to the popular demand to restrict immigration.

For the automotive industry, which has evolved into a complex integrated global production process, free movement of components in the production process and the individuals that provide those services is critical. In 2017 only 44% of the value of content for vehicles manufactured in the UK was supplied from inside the country (Holweg, Davies, & Wood, 2017). Changing the rules related to this interchange and imposing tariff calculations and cost on these components will make assembly in the UK less attractive. In addition, 80% of UK-assembled vehicles are exported. Increased tariffs on these products will hurt UK manufacturing. But beyond the basic issues of trade are complex rules related to how vehicles conform to safety and environmental regulations. These are highlighted in the White Paper using an example of vehicle type-approvals. The UK proposal is that the EU and the UK would accept each other's methods of testing and their documentation attesting conformity.

Unfortunately, the issue is much broader than the testing procedure. The entire set of regulatory requirements surrounding the motor industry serves as a price of entry condition for participation in trade. The issue that will be explored later in this text is how the UK will be forced to accept changes to the regulatory environment in which they no longer have a vote. Accepting the testing procedure is essentially comparable to the University of Strasbourg telling the University of Leeds that to accept a transfer student it would be willing to accept the scantrons for the student's exams as long as all the test questions were from Strasbourg. The UK automotive manufacturers risk being on the fringes of the industry in the near term and potentially excluded down the road. This risk is largely brushed off in the White Paper with statements regarding the EU and the UK starting from a position of trust in each other. That may be wishful thinking in the current environment.

The EU response to the UK proposals has been varied, and largely polite, but there has been little appetite to accept the abrogation of the Four Freedoms. In an Op-ed piece, Michel Barnier, the European Commission's Chief Brexit Negotiator was direct:

> The UK wants to leave our common regulatory area, where people, goods, services and capital move freely across national borders. These are the economic foundations on which the EU

was built...some UK proposals would undermine our Single Market which is one of the EU's biggest achievements. The UK wants to keep free movement of goods between us, but not of people and services. And it proposes to apply EU customs rules without being part of the EU's legal order. Thus, the UK wants to take back sovereignty and control of its own laws, which we respect, but it cannot ask the EU to lose control of its borders and laws.

(Barnier, 2018)

By the time this text is published, the UK will have passed the initial 29 March 2019 deadline for the breakup and the departure date has been rescheduled twice, with the UK now aiming at 31 October 2019 at the latest but still with a ratified withdrawal agreement which may or may not happen. It is difficult to predict the exact form that the agreements (or lack thereof) will take, but it is fairly clear that the UK will not have all of the flexibilities that it desires. The intent of this volume is to examine how Brexit is likely to impact the motor industry in the UK and its subsequent impact on the UK economy.

Draft proposal

The expectation was that a formal proposal for the withdrawal of the UK from the EU would solidify how the motor vehicle industry would be treated. Unfortunately, the 14 November 2018 draft proposal that the UK government submitted, and subsequently rejected by Parliament multiple times, was largely silent when it comes to vehicles (Lichfield, 2018). Thus, there is little that can be considered beyond the text in the White Paper to understand the post-Brexit impact on the motor vehicle industry.

It appears that the main impact of the Draft Agreement would be to kick the can down the road by establishing a transition period through 31 December 2020 when things will remain more or less the status quo (UK Government and European Union, 2018; Article 126). Unfortunately, as the draft agreement was not approved by Parliament, all this does is heighten the uncertainty the industry confronts, which will not be positive for UK vehicle manufacturing. Increasing the uncertainty, Article 3 of the agreement states "The United Kingdom... may at any time before 1 July 2020 request the extension of the transition period...". When vehicle manufacturers place investments of hundreds of millions of pounds, this is not the kind of language that instils confidence.

References

Barnier, M. (2018). *An ambitious partnership with the UK after Brexit*. Brussels: European Union. Retrieved from https://ec.europa.eu/commission/news/ambitious-partnership-uk-after-brexit-2018-aug-02_en

Carmona, J., Cîrlig, C.-C., & Sgueo, G. (2018). *Withdrawal from the European Union: legal and procedural issues*. Retrieved from http://www.europarl.europa.eu/RegData/etudes/IDAN/2017/599352/EPRS_IDA%282017%29599352_EN.pdf

Holweg, M., Davies, P., & Wood, M. (2017). *Growing the automotive supply chain: local vehicle content analysis*. Retrieved from https://www.automotivecouncil.co.uk/wp-content/uploads/sites/13/2017/06/Automotive-Council-UK-local-sourcing-content-research-2017-Final-1.pdf

Lichfield, J. (2018). The Brexiteers' 'take back our waters' pledge is meaningless hype. *The Guardian*. Retrieved from https://www.theguardian.com/commentisfree/2018/nov/23/brexit-waters-fishing-industry-eu?CMP=Share_iOSApp_Other

UK Government and European Union. (2018). *Draft Agreement on the withdrawal of the United Kingdom of Great Britain and Northern Ireland from the European Union and the European Atomic Energy Community*. Retrieved from https://ec.europa.eu/commission/publications/draft-agreement-withdrawal-united-kingdom-great-britain-and-northern-ireland-european-union-and-european-atomic-energy-community-agreed-negotiators-level-14-november-2018_en

UK Parliament. (2018). *The future relationship between the United Kingdom and the European Union*. London: Presented to Parliament by the Prime Minister by Command of Her Majesty. Retrieved from https://www.gov.uk/government/publications

3 Overview of the UK vehicle industry and its global position

The importance of the car industry, both to the UK economy and somehow to the global economy, was a recurring theme during the Brexit debate and has underpinned post-vote worries about the divorce negotiations. Long before the negotiations had really started between the UK Government and the EU even about the UK's departure let alone the future arrangements, in October 2016 the UK Government provided written guarantees to Nissan about the post-Brexit status of the industry in the UK when assurances were sought alongside considerations of where to locate car assembly operations. These assurances were then reported as being extended to all parts of the motor industry (Marr, 2016). Such assurances were conspicuously lacking for other industries, with even big economic players such as the financial services industry given little sense of what was likely to come through the negotiations and certainly no comfort letters. Subsequent press headlines maintain the special status of the car industry in the press: "UK car industry must be at the heart of Brexit negotiations, say MPs" (Monaghan, 2018); "No upside in Brexit for British car industry – lawmakers" (Pitas, 2018); "Brexit is killing investment in UK car industry" (Riley, 2018). It has become a cliché to say that the vehicle industry is important to the global economy, and the UK is an important part of that industry.

This chapter considers the global size of the car industry and the significance of the UK industry within it, considering what exactly is at risk in that sector. It argues that the data does not support the extent of the worries represented. While the motor industry is not unimportant, the broad trends facing it suggest significant challenges which dwarf the problems posed by Brexit. This is considered further in Chapter 8, but the argument in this chapter is that a greater sense of proportion is needed in the consideration of the significance of the car industry in the UK. This is not to say that the motor industry in

12 *Overview of the UK vehicle industry*

the UK is unimportant, only that among the industries that are likely to be harmed in Brexit, the vehicle industry is not the most significant.

The vehicle world picture

The magnitude of the global vehicle industry is astounding. Figure 3.1 shows that in 2017 there were slightly over 97 million cars, trucks and buses produced, 73% more than in 1990. If the auto industry worldwide were its own country, it would be the sixth largest global economy just behind the total size of the UK economy (OICA, 2017).[1] By far the greatest growth has been in China where in 2017 more than 29 million vehicles were produced compared to only 1.8 million in 1990. China today represents 30% of the global vehicle total compared with 3% in 1990. The increase in China represents two-thirds of all vehicle production growth since the turn of the century, and China's increase in production has been larger than today's size of any other region (OICA, 2017). Thus, it is not surprising that the vehicle industry drives much of the discussion around global business.

Exports of vehicles are also a substantial component of global business. The value of car exports in 2017 was almost $750 billion

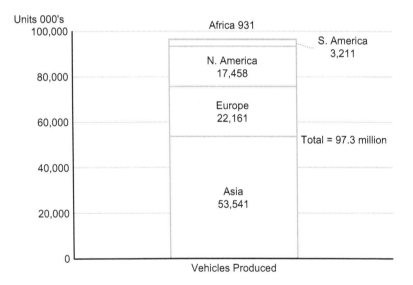

Figure 3.1 Global vehicle production – 2017.
Source: OICA.

Overview of the UK vehicle industry 13

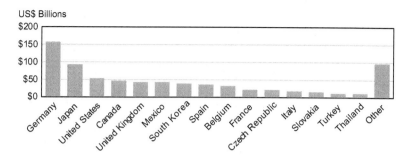

Figure 3.2 2017 Car exports by country of origin.
Source: worldstopexport.com.

(Workman, n.d.). Figure 3.2 shows passenger car exports from the fifteen largest exporting countries. Lorries tend to be exported in low numbers, because they are expensive to ship. It is worth noting that as yet China is not a player of significance in the export of vehicles.

In 2017 China accounted for only 1% of car exports, ranking them only 20th among manufacturing nations. This is a situation that is likely to change soon. In part the low China numbers are related to the fact that much of the production in China has been made by international automakers who have little interest in challenging exports from their home markets. As the domestic Chinese manufacturers expand and satisfy more of the local demand, however, there is no question that the Chinese will become major export players in vehicles. As China vehicle exports grow, exports of vehicles from the EU, and the UK, will face stiffer competition.

The global automotive industry is also a major employer, although not to the extent that it was following World War II through the middle of the 20th century. In fact, employment levels in vehicle manufacturing plants have been declining for some time. As an illustration, in 1996 Hyundai UK ran an advertisement that boasted "Last year Hyundai produced 1.1 million cars. The workforce built 3% of them…97% of the work on our production line is carried out by state of the art robots" (Wood, 1996, p. 40). The use of robots has only increased since then. However, the industry does remain a source of significant jobs. The International Organization of Motor Vehicle Manufacturers (OICA) estimates that it takes direct labour of more than eight people per vehicle produced, and five times that many in indirect labour for distribution and service provision. A separate engineering firm estimate suggests more than 11 people per vehicle produced are engaged in

14 *Overview of the UK vehicle industry*

direct employment (Wickham, 2017). Overall, the OICA estimates that the vehicle industry represents more than 5% of global manufacturing employment (OICA, 2017). However, much of the world's vehicle manufacturing is relatively low scale, and as a result skews the employment totals. Production is more efficient in the major manufacturing sites in Europe. For example, the direct labour required per vehicle produced in Spain is only 8.7 workers; in the UK and Germany 8.5 (Wickham, 2017). With this global overview, we now turn to examining the position of the industry in Europe.

Europe vehicle scale

The 22 million vehicles that Europe produced in 2017 represent 23% of the global total and is spread across 25 countries. Only nine of those countries, the ones detailed in Figure 3.3, each have production that exceeds 1 million units. The fifteen countries labelled as 'Other Europe' combine for production of 2.8 million units with some producing as few as 10,000 vehicles annually. Eighty-five percent of the European total is produced in EU countries, while the UK accounts for 8%.

The five largest EU producers, Germany, Spain, France, UK and Italy, directly employ more than 1.8 million workers in the automotive industry. In terms of trade, European countries exported the majority of international vehicle sales at 54.8% amounting to £300 billion in value. Europe's exports were more than double the next largest region, Asia, which had 23.6% of export vehicle sales (Workman, n.d.).

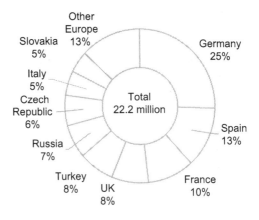

Figure 3.3 Europe vehicle production – 2017.
Source: OICA.

British auto industry background[2]

The mass market for cars started in the 1950s and 1960s following World War II. In 1950 the UK produced 785,000 vehicles and it would seem that Britain was poised to become a major global player in the industry. By 1960 the UK industry had increased by 130% (Wood, 1996). In contrast, Japan had virtually no vehicle industry. Following the war, Japan was only allowed to produce a limited number of trucks, and Toyota went bankrupt. The company was saved by receiving contracts for military vehicles and repair parts during the Korean conflict. Total production in 1953 was only 10,000 units. But, in the 1960s the UK automotive industry was wracked by poor management, union militancy and government interference. This book does not pretend to assign blame for what is still a hotly debated issue, only to note that these problems posed a significant and negative impact on the industry. The UK vehicle industry entered a prolonged period of restrictive practices and wildcat strikes. This resulted in a failure to invest in new plant and equipment that by the mid-1960s left British vehicles with a reputation as "unreliable, leaky, cranky beasts" (Jacobs, 2018). This image recalls for this author an experience during the 1970s when I purchased a used MG Midget. Before buying the vehicle, I took it to the local mechanic for an inspection. I was concerned that when I parked the vehicle it left a spot of oil on the pavement. I recall vividly the mechanic telling me "Hell, if it didn't leak oil it wouldn't be British".

By the late 1960s the situation had become so serious that the Labour Government, as part of its effort to modernise industry through the Industrial Reorganisation Corporation, consolidated 20 automotive brands into the British Leyland Motor Company. Consolidating a collection of failing companies into a mega corporation rarely increases efficiency, and ultimately the firm was essentially nationalised after a multi-billion pound government bail-out in 1975. UK car production had peaked in 1972 at 1.92 million units, a volume that has yet to be achieved again (ONS, 2004; SMMT, 2018).

The decline of the major car makers was inevitably accompanied by a collapse of major portions of the supply chain. Component and sub-assembly manufacturing, foundries as well as steel and aluminium production all deteriorated. Meanwhile, during the late 1960s the Japanese (and German) auto industries flourished. Perhaps because their industrial infrastructure was levelled during the war, these nations invested in new efficient production facilities, and importantly benefitted from

16 *Overview of the UK vehicle industry*

the production of new generations of smaller fuel-efficient engines that gained major popularity during the 1973 oil crisis. Thus, the 1970s was a lost decade for the UK vehicle industry, and by 1984 vehicle production had declined to about two-thirds of the 1960 level (ONS, 2004; SMMT, 2018).

From that low point the industry began a renaissance. Ironically, it was the Japanese, beginning with Honda, that initiated the recovery. Honda was induced by the Thatcher Government to form a joint venture with Rover. This was less than successful as the companies were culturally incompatible, and the Japanese insisted on importing their own quality control, productivity levels and management processes, but it was a beginning. It was, however, the 1984 agreement with Nissan that led to a major plant on the site of the former Sunderland airfield. Nissan chose the UK because of a combination of government incentives, a readily available workforce in a depressed area and good access to ports and airports (Kelly, 2013).

From that point the UK vehicle industry has transformed and grown with the addition of new manufacturers and models. The Indian conglomerate Tata bought the Land Rover and Jaguar marques from Ford in 2008 and has invested heavily in the UK. Today, as detailed in Table 3.1, there are 35 assembly plants in the UK producing vehicles and engines, and while a number of those are low-volume sports cars and commercial vehicle assembly operations, the industry has recovered substantially.

Unfortunately, the lost opportunities during the 1950s, 1960s and 1970s have meant the UK had to compete its way back against now well-established international competition. In 2017 the UK produced 1.75 million vehicles; Japan produced five and a half times that volume (JAMA, 2018). If the UK had avoided its self-inflicted pain and developed the competitive advantage it had at the end of World War II, it perhaps could be a 10 million a year manufacturing centre.

Table 3.1 UK Vehicle Assembly Plants

	Cars	Lt Comm Veh	Trucks/ Buses	Engines	Total
Assembly Plants	20	1	6	8	35

Source: ACEA.

UK manufacturing

Beyond vehicles, manufacturing as a whole has declined as a share of the UK economy. In 1948 manufacturing represented 48% of the UK's Gross Domestic Product (GDP) (ONS, 2016). In 2017 that share was 10% (ONS, 2018a). The absolute number of employees in manufacturing has declined by 60% over the last 30 years. In contrast, as Figure 3.4 shows, employment in services over the same timeframe has risen more than 70%.

The fact is that the UK economy has become, like most developed countries, service based as shown in Figure 3.5. The component shares bounce around a bit from year to year, but in comparison, the share of GDP from services is 79% in France, 69% in Germany and 78% in the US (ONS, 2016).[3]

However, this does not mean that UK manufacturing output declined absolutely, only that the service sector grew more rapidly. Office for National Statistics (ONS) data displayed in Figure 3.6 show that the real value of manufacturing production in the UK grew 6% from 1990 through 2017, despite a decline during the financial crisis. However, the service sector nearly doubled during the same period (ONS, 2018a).

The vehicle portion of UK manufacturing has recently mirrored what has been happening to manufacturing as a whole. Following the lost decade of the 1970s significant investments by foreign manufacturers resulted in a solid recovery in vehicle production during the 1980s as

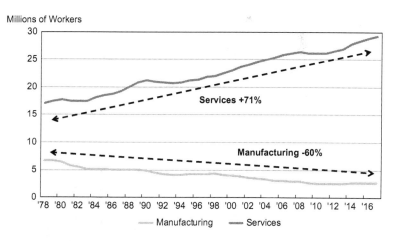

Figure 3.4 UK manufacturing and service sector employment.
Source: ONS.

18 *Overview of the UK vehicle industry*

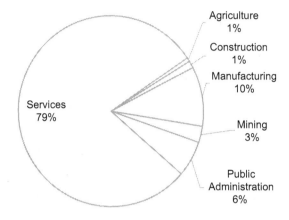

Figure 3.5 UK 2017 GDP by sector.
Source: ONS.

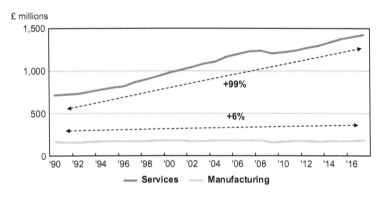

Figure 3.6 UK services & manufacturing real values 1990–2017.
Source: ONS.

shown in Figure 3.7. To be fair to the industry, domestic production was hurt in the first part of this century by a strong pound between 1997 and 2007. In addition, there was a significant downturn during the financial crisis, but production recovered during the last decade. Importantly, UK production quality has made substantial improvements as is indicated by the fact that 80% of UK manufactured cars are exported (SMMT, 2018). This could never have happened if the industrial unrest of earlier decades had persisted.

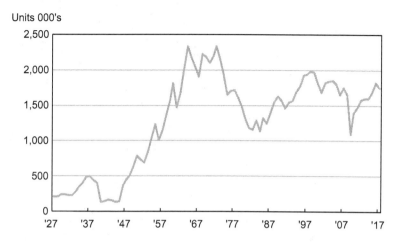

Figure 3.7 UK vehicle production.
Sources: ONS, SMMT.

As production grew, the value of motor vehicles as a portion of manufacturing output increased, however, the general downward trend of manufacturing in the overall economy continued. Figure 3.8a shows the vehicle share of total manufacturing GDP hovered around 7% in the 1990s, fell to 5% during the financial crisis, but recovered to 9% in 2017. That increase was facilitated by additional UK investment commitments totalling £7 billion between 2011 and 2013 by most of the major manufacturers including Jaguar Land Rover, BMW, Nissan, Honda and Vauxhall (Monaghan, 2014; Warner, 2012). Despite that positive news for vehicle manufacturing, Figure 3.8b shows that the total manufacturing component of the economy continued to slide over the last quarter century to its current 10% level. Finally, to put the vehicle manufacturing industry into perspective, Figure 3.8c shows that the manufacturing component of this industry has generally declined, and from a Brexit impact perspective is well less than 1% of GDP. One percent of GDP is not insignificant, and it represents an important number of jobs, but a potential decline of the manufacturing component of the industry does not represent a crisis.

More important to the overall economy than the manufacturing portion of the motor industry is the service element. The wholesale and retail trade and repair of motor vehicles category is counted in the national income accounts as a service, not manufacturing, and as Figure 3.9 shows it is twice as large as the manufacturing component. This, of course,

20 *Overview of the UK vehicle industry*

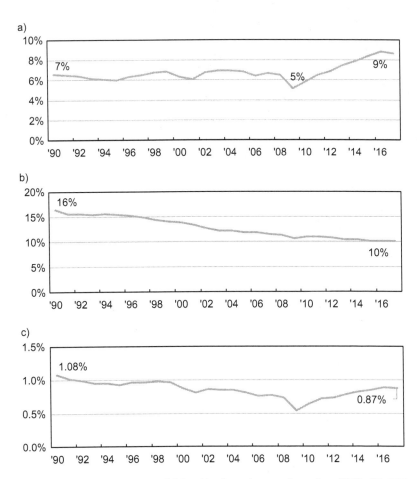

Figure 3.8 (a) UK motor vehicles % of total manufacturing GDP. (b) UK manufacturing % of total GDP. (c) UK motor vehicles % of total GDP.
Source: ONS.

expands the visibility and attention the industry receives. It also must be recognised that regardless of what happens to vehicle manufacturing post-Brexit, people will still purchase vehicles, and those vehicles will need to be serviced. This portion of the industry is somewhat insulated from the Brexit risk; imported repair parts will become more expensive if borders are no longer open, but the actual service elements are primarily local and would be unaffected by customs issues.

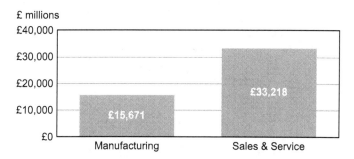

Figure 3.9 UK 2017 GDP component of motor vehicles.
Source: ONS.

Even with all of the growth in recent vehicle production, the combined total of manufacturing and service in the motor vehicle industry has not reached 3% of the UK GDP in the last quarter century. This is a little over a third of the size of the financial and insurance industry, and only a fifth the size of real estate. Again, this does not mean that the motor industry is insignificant, only that its value to the economy, and the Brexit debate, must be placed in context.

The industry, like manufacturing in general, has also become less of an employment factor. There are several reasons for this: extensive automation thus increasing productivity, rising real wages which induced manufacturers to shift production to lower-cost locations, the relatively strong pound from 1997 to 2007, which amplified the wage gap, and the expansion of other industrial nations' capacity, particularly China, India and South Korea. The increase in productivity in the industry must not be underestimated. Experimental Office of National Statistics data tracking UK productivity shown in Figure 3.10 reveals that following the financial crisis, which hurt manufacturing across the board, between the first quarter of 1999 and the first quarter of 2018, vehicle manufacturing increased productivity by 66%, compared, for example, with productivity in financial services that grew less than 1% (ONS, 2018b). The growth in productivity has been generated by a number of factors. Increased computerisation of many elements of the production process has combined with techniques like lean manufacturing, 6-Sigma and Total Quality Management which have all played a significant role, while increased outsourcing of lower-value-added activities to low-cost countries has concentrated higher-value-adding activities in developed economies like the UK (Price Waterhouse Coopers, 2009).

22 Overview of the UK vehicle industry

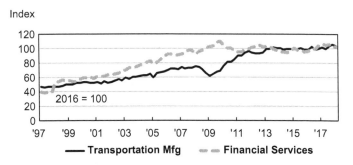

Figure 3.10 Productivity index UK transportation manufacturing & financial services.
Source: Office of National Statistics.

This means fewer functions performed in developed countries, but those activities that remain add higher value.

This productivity increase is an important element in understanding how the vehicle industry works. The motor industry is a high fixed cost, high variable profit business. Contemporary vehicle plants are large-scale operations. While it is difficult to generalise, particularly when you compare economy versus up-level vehicles, but in general, the minimum size of a vehicle plant producing a single model is about 250,000 units per year. It is not uncommon for factories to assemble more than 100 cars per hour. Hyundai states that its plant in Ulsan, South Korea produces one vehicle every 20 seconds (Hyundai, 2018). In decades past a firm could operate plants at smaller scale with more manual labour and slower supply lines. Today, just-in-time productivity requires components and subassemblies to arrive at an assembly site within a small window which means they must be located relatively close to the final assembly point. Then, producing a large number of the same model necessitates substantial exports since consumers want variety.

Over time the increased technology and productivity of the industry required production to be concentrated where markets are large and export potential is strong. It used to be that virtually every nation wanted its own vehicle assembly industry as an indication of industrial strength. However, as examined later in this text, countries including Australia and New Zealand have ceased domestic production in favour of lower prices for consumers. And, it should be pointed out that each of those nations managed to survive economically. Countries like South Africa that continue to protect local assembly to maintain employment must restrict imports and struggle with consumer complaints about high vehicle prices.

Increased productivity does, however, impact labour. In 2017 the UK automotive industry employed 186,000 workers directly in manufacturing (SMMT, 2018). This compares with 502,000 in 1971 (Brown & Rhodes, 2018, p. 6). In recent times, employment declined from over 200,000 in 1999 to about 125,000 in 2010 before beginning a recovery to its present level (Brown & Rhodes, 2018, p. 6). Overall, however, vehicle industry direct employment represents only 1% of total UK employment. Yet many commentators remain seriously concerned about the fate of the vehicle industry in a post-Brexit environment. There are several reasons for this high level of anxiety including the industry's visibility, the number and widespread distribution of jobs supported by the industry and the industry's effort to make sure its position is heard.

Generating support above its weight

Vehicles are an industry that is apparent every day to virtually everyone. The UK is filled with roads that contain millions of cars, trucks and buses.

Figure 3.11 shows that there are nearly 40 million vehicles on UK roads (SMMT, 2018), almost exactly the same as the number of fully licensed drivers in the country (RAC, 2018). Eighty-seven percent of all vehicles are passenger cars, although it may seem at times like the roads are clogged with larger vehicles. As a consequence, vehicles are a part of almost everyone's daily life. Thus, the motor industry has greater visual impact than many others that have larger economic impact.

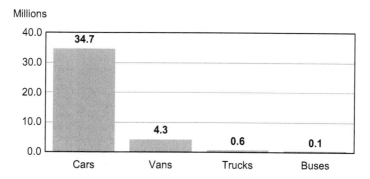

Figure 3.11 Vehicles on UK roads 2017.
Source: SMMT.

24 Overview of the UK vehicle industry

The industry also has an emotional impact on consumers. The brands of historic British cars are perhaps the strongest of any in the world. Even though they have transitioned to foreign ownership, the marques Aston Martin, Bentley, Jaguar, Land Rover, Lotus, MG, Mini, Rolls-Royce and Triumph to name a few are more than names, they evoke a history of British in the national psyche. There are few products to which consumers have greater attachment than their cars. This means that any change that impacts the industry will receive attention.

Another reason the industry gets wide visibility beyond its direct employment is that manufacturing jobs traditionally support a significant number of additional positions in an economy. Beyond the 186,000 UK motor industry direct jobs, there are another 630,000 indirect employees across the country (SMMT, 2018). These jobs are related to designing, engineering, selling, repairing and producing components. There are more than 66,000 UK businesses involved in these ancillary activities (Foxall, 2012). And these jobs do not include workers in industries such as the oil industry which would be a fraction of its size were it not for vehicles.

Automotive employment is also distributed throughout the country, which means that there is a vested interest across the nation in maintaining those jobs. Figure 3.12 shows that every Nomenclature of Territorial Units for Statistics (NUTS) as defined by the Office for National Statistics has direct automotive industry employment except Northern Ireland. The largest share is in the West Midlands, but there is enough volume in each region to indicate that those businesses will be vocal if jobs are at risk.

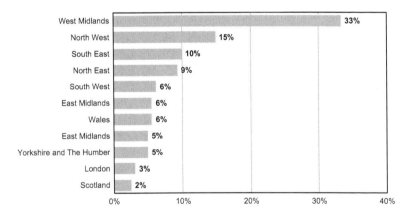

Figure 3.12 Percent of direct automotive employment by NUTS1 region.
Source: House of Commons, The motor industry: statistics and policy.

Overview of the UK vehicle industry 25

The industry also has a history of being vocal about its interests. Each year The Society of Motor Manufacturers & Traders (SMMT) issues and widely distributes reports on the level of production, employment and importance of the industry. Recently, they have been forceful in their warnings about risks to employment in the face of Brexit. In a position paper, the SMMT highlighted substantial risks to the industry, and thus its employment in five areas: (1) potential loss of the single market, (2) loss of competitiveness through potential higher customs tariffs and bureaucracy, (3) the lack of access to employment talent through restricted movement of labour, (4) the potential for extensive regulations outside the customs union and (5) the risk of losing exports, and hence employment (SMMT, 2017). The SMMT specifically warns that the price of an imported new vehicle in a post Brexit situation having to pay EU customs would rise by an average of £1,500. In what *The Guardian* reported as "the starkest warning yet from a single business sector" at a full day International Automotive Summit in London in June 2018, BMW warned that it may close its UK manufacturing sites in Cowley, Oxford, and Vauxhall said that the future of the Astra plant in Ellesmere Port is at risk if the industry is disadvantaged because of Brexit (O'Carroll & Topham, 2018). Even more recent, and immanent, are announcements by Ford and Jaguar Land Rover (JLR) that they are cutting thousands of European jobs. While the Ford announcement said that the cuts were not the result of Brexit, the JLR press release indicated that Brexit played an "indirect role" (Howard, 2019; Milligan & Garcia Perez, 2019). Both automakers indicated that the risks of Brexit uncertainty posed a threat.

The industry also has strong support in government. The House of Commons Business, Energy, and Industrial Strategy Committee bluntly warned that the potential shift of auto manufacturing to countries within the EU customs union could result in UK job losses in "the hundreds of thousands" (House of Commons Business, 2018). The same government report emphasised that "The Government has placed the automotive sector at the heart of its Industrial Strategy...". This support ensures that the motor industry receives substantial consideration in the Brexit negotiations.

Export component

As late as the end of the 1980s, European vehicle manufacturers sold the bulk of their output in their home markets. Renault and Peugeot sold largely in France, Opel and VW in Germany, Fiat in

26 *Overview of the UK vehicle industry*

Italy. A history of high tariffs in the 1930s combined with non-tariff barriers at borders and a focus on domestic redevelopment in the 1950s and 1960s led exports to be something of an afterthought. In fact, the US company General Motors actually had its highest year of vehicle exports in 1928 just before the Great Depression (Sloan, 1964). In part because of the scale economies mentioned above requiring large assembly plants, but also because of changing economics, the focus on exports has changed in a big way. The 1993 Maastricht treaty concept entrenching the 'four freedoms' of the movement of goods, services, people and money altered the thinking of a lot of industries, and the motor industry took full advantage of the opening.

Today, it is actually difficult to confidently state that vehicles in the EU are manufactured in a country. While the statistics say that 8 out of every 10 vehicles manufactured in the UK are exported, in a significant way this is an overstatement (SMMT, 2018). The vehicle industry has become global. UK-sourced components from tier one suppliers (the largest component manufacturers) in car manufacturing was only 44%. The balance came from outside the UK. While this was an increase from 36% in 2011, nevertheless a car that is produced in the UK is actually less than half made in the country (Holweg, Davies, & Wood, 2017). This is not unusual. The same study that identified the current local content estimated that there is globally a 60% maximum of local content in any major vehicle operation. This is a result of the dispersion of the suppler industry and the need for truly large-scale production of components that are similar across manufacturers and products.

The UK motor industry bottom line

All the above demonstrates that whether the UK motor industry is a dominant force in the economy or not, it is at risk if complex supply chains and trade economics are disrupted. So, the conclusion before moving into the impact of Brexit on the motor industry is that it is actually incorrect to say that the UK has an automotive industry. What the UK has is participation in a global activity that produces about a 100 million vehicles a year; a process that transcends national borders and is critically interdependent on activities that occur in many countries. The five leading vehicle manufacturers in the UK: Jaguar Land Rover, Nissan, BMW, Honda and Toyota are all foreign owned. This same dispersion is occurring in other industries, but the complexity of a car and the sheer number of components that go into its production make this industry stand out as a risk for Brexit. Whatever the form Brexit takes, the UK government will have to determine if continued participation in the production of cars is a 'red line' that is essential to maintain. Any structure that slows global logistics will require government support of some kind to offset the resulting cost penalties. We have seen in this chapter that there are important constituencies that will push for such support. Those must be considered as one of the consequences of Brexit.

Notes

1 Elsewhere in this text there is mention that if California were an independent economy it would be the fifth largest globally, but in the global calculations the UK remains the fifth largest.
2 This history draws heavily on two short but excellent histories of the UK auto industry. The first is by Jeremy Warner published in *The Telegraph* on 11 August, 2012, https://www.telegraph.co.uk/finance/comment/jeremy-warner/9468981/How-Britain-won-the-global-car-war.html. The second is a blog by Michael Jacobs from January 2018, https://www.quora.com/What-happened-to-the-British-car-and-the-motorcycle-industry.
3 For comparison, the manufacturing component of GDP in Japan is 21% https://globaledge.msu.edu/countries/japan/memo.

References

Brown, J., & Rhodes, C. (2018). *Motor industry: statistics and policy.* London. Retrieved from https://researchbriefings.parliament.uk/ResearchBriefing/Summary/SN00611#fullreport
Foxall, J. (2012). *UK car economy in numbers.* Retrieved from https://www.telegraph.co.uk/motoring/news/9541721/UK-car-economy-in-numbers.html
Holweg, M., Davies, P., & Wood, M. (2017). *Growing the automotive supply chain: local vehicle content analysis.* Retrieved from https://www.automotivecouncil.co.uk/wp-content/uploads/sites/13/2017/06/Automotive-Council-UK-local-sourcing-content-research-2017-Final-1.pdf
House of Commons Business, E., and Industrial Strategy Committee. (2018). *The impact of Brexit on the automotive sector.* London. Retrieved from https://publications.parliament.uk/pa/cm201719/cmselect/cmbeis/379/37904.htm#_idTextAnchor002
Howard, P. W. (2019). Ford to cut thousands of jobs in turnaround plan. *Detroit Free Press.* Retrieved from https://www.freep.com/story/money/cars/2019/01/10/ford-job-cuts-volkswagen/2534463002/
Hyundai. (2018). *About us: history.* Retrieved from https://www.hyundai.co.uk/about-us/think-you-know-hyundai/history
Jacobs, M. (2018). *What happened to the British car and the motorcycle industry?* Retrieved from https://www.quora.com/What-happened-to-the-British-car-and-the-motorcycle-industry

28 *Overview of the UK vehicle industry*

JAMA. (2018). *Japanese Automobile and Motorcycle Industry Statistics*. Retrieved from http://www.jama.org/japanese-automobile-and-motorcycle-industry-statistics/

Kelly, M. (2013). *Looking back at Nissan's 25 years of success*. 25 June. Retrieved from http://www.thejournal.co.uk/news/north-east-news/looking-back-nissans-25-years-4424562

Marr, A. (2016). The Andrew Marr Show. In: *BBC*: https://www.bbc.co.uk/programmes/b081wrqg.

Milligan, E., & Garcia Perez, I. (2019). Jaguar to Slash 4,500 Jobs in Brexit Slump, Joining Ford in Cuts. *bloomberg.com*. Retrieved from https://www.bloomberg.com/news/articles/2019-01-10/jaguar-says-it-will-cut-4-500-jobs-worldwide-amid-brexit-slump

Monaghan, A. (2014). UK car production will surpass record 1970s level by 2017, says trade body. *The Guardian*. Retrieved from https://www.theguardian.com/business/2014/jan/07/uk-car-production-surpass-1972-record-2017

Monaghan, A. (2018). UK car industry must be at the heart of Brexit negotiations, say MPs. *The Guardian*. Retrieved from https://www.theguardian.com/business/2018/mar/01/uk-car-industry-must-be-at-the-heart-of-brexit-negotiations-say-mps

O'Carroll, L., & Topham, G. (2018). Brexit uncertainty puts thousands of jobs at risk, car industry warns. *The Guardian*. Retrieved from https://www.theguardian.com/politics/2018/jun/26/brexit-uncertainty-putting-860000-jobs-at-risk-warns-car-industry

OICA. (2017). *Sales and production statistics*. Retrieved from http://www.oica.net/category/production-statistics/2012-statistics/

ONS. (2004). *Motor vehicle production*. London: Office for National Statistics: The National Archive. Retrieved from http://www.statistics.gov.uk/statbase/Product.asp?vlnk=172

ONS. (2016). *Five facts about the UK service sector*. London. Retrieved from https://www.ons.gov.uk/economy/economicoutputandproductivity/output/articles/fivefactsabouttheukservicesector/2016-09-29

ONS. (2018a). *Gross Domestic Product*. Retrieved from https://www.ons.gov.uk/economy/grossdomesticproductgdp/datasets/ukgdpolowlevelaggregates

ONS. (2018b). *Productivity Index*. Retrieved from https://www.ons.gov.uk/economy/economicoutputandproductivity/productivitymeasures

Pitas, C. (2018). No upside in Brexit for British car industry-lawmakers. *Reuters*. Retrieved from https://www.reuters.com/article/britain-eu-autos/no-upside-in-brexit-for-british-car-industry-lawmakers-idUSL8N1QI3PY

Price Waterhouse Coopers. (2009). *The future of UK manufacturing: reports of its death are greatly exaggerated*. Retrieved from https://www.pwc.co.uk/assets/pdf/ukmanufacturing-300309.pdf

RAC. (2018). *Motoring FAQ*. Retrieved from https://www.racfoundation.org/motoring-faqs/mobility

Riley, C. (2018). Brexit is killing investment in UK car industry. *CNN Money*. Retrieved from https://money.cnn.com/2018/06/26/news/economy/brexit-uk-car-manufacturing-bmw/index.html

Sloan, A. P. J. (1964). *My years with General Motors.* New York: Doubleday & Company, Inc.

SMMT. (2017). *Delivering UK automotive Brexit priorities.* Retrieved from https://www.smmt.co.uk/industry-topics/brexit/delivering-uk-automotive-brexit-priorities/

SMMT. (2018). *Motor industry facts 2018.* London. Retrieved from https://www.smmt.co.uk/reports/smmt-motor-industry-facts-2018/

Warner, J. (2012). How Britain won the global car war. *The Guardian.* Retrieved from https://www.telegraph.co.uk/finance/comment/jeremy-warner/9468981/How-Britain-won-the-global-car-war.html

Wickham, A. (2017). *The Automotive industry employs more people than you think.* Retrieved from https://www.fircroft.com/blogs/the-automotive-industry-employs-more-people-than-you-think-71462610395

Wood, J. (1996). *Motor Industry of Britain Centenary Book.* London: Eclat Initiatives Ltd.

Workman, D. (n.d.) *Car exports by country.* Retrieved from http://www.worldstopexports.com/car-exports-country/

4 EU market regulation affecting motor vehicles

Product standards and rules of origin

Cars and the motor industry operate in a highly regulated space. Relevant rules range from permissions as to the use of vehicles to product standards and the more generalised frameworks that apply to the manufacture and sale of any product. Cars and car use have a distinct category of offences applicable to them; the way societies distinguish the misuse of vehicles from other misuses tells us something about the special status of cars and car use.

In the EU, vehicle standards have long been set both to facilitate the free market and the production and trade in vehicles, and to achieve air quality improvements. This was true even before environmental protection aims otherwise featured in the EU legal system. While it may be that the association of cars with environmental pollution has not always determined the regulation of cars, the association of regulatory standards applicable to vehicles and environmental standards is now close. The EU has historically been pretty precise in determining the standards applicable to motor vehicles. This is not an area of legislation in the model of general frameworks. In fact, vehicle and engine standards in the EU are specific when compared to other product standard requirements. This chapter explores the regulatory regime as it currently operates and considers the extent to which the setting of a standard for this product – the motor vehicle – in the EU frames vehicle production. One of the main problems with ignoring such EU standards, for cars as much as for any other product, is that while there is the possibility to produce to different standards, those seeking to sell cars in the EU market still need to meet the standards requirements in that market. So, this chapter argues that the standardised regime defining a motor vehicle and its emissions will continue to have great significance to UK producers. The subsequent chapter considers internationally applicable standards to reinforce this point, but this chapter focusses on determining EU applicable standards.

The arguments put forward to justify the highly regulated environment applicable to the car industry tend to locate themselves in concerns about how the market would operate if left alone. The externalities that arise from car use, most specifically air pollution emitted from vehicles, impose a cost which is not factored into production or use costs without an intervention to ensure they are counted (Coase, 1960). But, in fact, the starting point for EU product standards was as much about coordinating and harmonising standards that already existed in the participating States than it was about imposing a new body of rules. The initial legislative efforts on vehicle and engine emissions – similarly to the development of other product standards – were developed in conjunction with initiatives to build the European common market. Common standards for vehicles enabled German car manufacturers to sell their cars in France in fair competition with French vehicle manufacturers. The idea around vehicle standards was that regulation supported market forces in the car market by removing (national) barriers in (international) markets. This instance of history in the car industry was no doubt rather particular to the combination of growth in the car market at the same time as European economic integration was such a politically popular focus, but the size and influence of European car manufacturers meant the products resulting from the European market framework had an impact in other markets where their industry was growing without also being part of the creation of the wider international market. BMWs were compared to Fords even before US consumers bought many, and BMWs were being built to European Community, rather than different German standards, as early as the 1960s.

One of the interesting features of cars as a product is the extent to which a single vehicle is in fact a composite of parts, some basic and some highly technical, and many produced by different manufacturers. Vehicle production then is often characterised as an assembly operation, and the supply chain for vehicle components is both of great significance to vehicle producers and high profile as an issue caused by Brexit. Parts for cars made in any Member State could come from all over the EU, and this is as much true of cars assembled in the northeast of England as it is of cars made in Bavaria. This chapter goes on to consider how the EU rules of origin apply to supply chains and finished products, specifically by reference to the vehicle industry. The determining of rules of origin largely was set as the common market was established in the 1960s – it is associated with the establishment of the customs union and constitutes an important component on the law abolishing tariffs between Member States in the internal market. This

32   *EU market regulation affecting motor vehicles*

section will focus on the effect, or potential effect, of the UK exiting the EU on the ability of UK-based vehicle manufacturers to continue to trade with EU Member States as well as countries outside the EU – third countries – due in a large part to rules of origin.

More latterly, there has been a marked shift from a focus on product and engine standards to initiatives managing the use of vehicles. This reflects a recognition of the abiding popularity of the private car despite the broader social and environmental concerns about vehicle numbers and their associated impact. Also, product and/or engine standards have in any case been shown to have a number of limitations. For example, the specific choice of measures, generally focused on particular pollutants, and the science around which pollutants are 'bad' is not and probably cannot be fixed. Understandings change all the time, and only a few years ago diesel was seen as a cleaner fuel, largely because of the possibilities of achieving greater distances of travel per unit of diesel when compared to possible distances with petrol. This meant a regulatory choice as to which pollutants would consequently be the focus of engine standards regulation, which meant an air quality focus on CO_2 rather than particulates. Subsequently, this choice has been seen to be a poor one as the science now again shows diesel is dirtier than petrol.

The big limitation with using car engine standards as a primary tool in the combat of air pollution is rather obviously that limiting emissions will not have the impact sought where there is exponential growth in the overall number of (ever cleaner) vehicles. And then, a focus on particular pollutants associates the environmental issues with cars that pollute, but does nothing about other sustainability concerns, in particular the social and economic aspects of sustainable development. For example, emission standards do nothing about congestion, or indeed more general social or economic problems. It is a targeted solution addressing a specific problem; unfortunately the problems are broad.

This chapter also introduces the close relationship between EU and UN requirements. Broadly, we argue that the EU standards are largely inescapable in the UK when it comes to export options. Whatever independence in decision-making is achieved by Brexit, all that will happen is that the UK will be required to adhere to international requirements and its voice will get lost in the setting of these standards.

Rules of origin

The free movement of goods is arguably one of the great accomplishments of the European endeavour; one of the four fundamental freedoms, it is the driving force behind the creation, development and maintenance of the internal market. As of the date of withdrawal, the UK will cease to be part of the internal market and accordingly will terminate participation in the freedom of movement of goods. The UK may no longer avail itself of the EU preferential trade arrangements with third countries and will itself become a third country vis-à-vis the EU. Whilst this is likely to have substantial and far-reaching consequences for many UK-based industries, certain idiosyncrasies of the automotive industry intensify the magnitude of this already significant paradigm shift.

Though uncertainty regarding the details of any Brexit deal persists, it is submitted that, irrespective of any preferential trade agreement likely to be achieved, the UK automotive industry will be unable to comply with preferential rule of origin requirements.

> In the event that the UK and the EU does not have a Free Trade Agreement (FTA) in place in a 'no deal' scenario, trade with the EU will be on non-preferential, World Trade Organisation terms. This means that Most Favoured Nation (MFN) tariffs and non-preferential rules of origin would apply to consignments between the UK and EU.
>
> (HM Revenue & Customs, 2018)

The Treaty on the Functioning of the European Union (TFEU) ensures that free movement applies to all goods that originate in the EU or are brought legally into circulation in the EU (European Union, 2012; Article 30; subsequent references will refer to TFEU), with the Court of Justice of the European Union defining 'goods' as products which 'can be valued in money and which are capable, as such, of forming the subject of commercial transactions' (European Communities, 2006). Article 28 TFEU states:

> The Union shall comprise a customs union which shall cover all trade in goods and which shall involve the prohibition between Member States of customs duties on imports and exports and of all charges having equivalent effect, and the adoption of a common customs tariff in their relations with third countries.

There are, in theory, no tariffs on products traded between EU Member States, with imports from third countries to EU Member States – that is, across the EU's external border – being regulated by the EU's Common Customs Tariff. Post-Brexit, the UK will be free to impose its own version of a customs tariff and will be free of:

34 *EU market regulation affecting motor vehicles*

- Prohibitions on financial restrictions of custom duties and charges having equivalent effect (TFEU, Article 30)
- Taxation which restricts free movement (TFEU, Article 10)
- Non-financial quantitative restrictions and measures that have equivalent effect (TFEU, Article 34, Article 35).

Whilst extracting the UK from this regime for some chimes with the pro-Brexit notion of 'taking back control', leaving the EU has serious implications for future UK trade with both the EU and third countries. Naturally, the UK will be free to negotiate its own trade deals and be placed in a position to impose tariff and non-tariff barriers in order to protect its own industries. Of course, the reverse is also true; other countries or customs unions, most notably the EU, will be free to do the same vis-à-vis UK exports. With the EU's current external tariff on cars at 10% (or 6.5% for developing countries) and tariffs of vehicle components ranging from 2.5% to 4%, the "introduction of UK-EU tariffs would be hugely damaging to UK automotive...put[ting] the UK at an immediate competitive disadvantage" (Comments of Society of Motor Manufacturers and Traders, House of Lords, 2017). Aside from the clear detriment of being subject to tariff barriers, the equally significant impediment of non-tariff barriers surface due to the notion of rules of origin.

Rules of origin are defined as laws, regulations, norms, provisions or other legal tools used to determine the country of origin of goods (WTO, 1994). Despite efforts at the WTO, there is no single 'rule' of origin. Rather, countries are free to apply their own, substantively disparate 'rules' of origin; setting the test of nationality as they wish, much as the issuance of passports is determined by each individual state, according to their own rules. Nations use these rules for a variety of purposes, including the compiling of trade statistics, for labelling and marking requirements and (WTO, 2019), most importantly for present purposes, to determine if a good or product is to be considered "sufficiently linked to the exporting country to count as originating there" (Holmes & Jacob, 2018, p. 2). A product that is not deemed sufficiently linked will not be able to benefit from any preferential trade agreement.

Broadly, goods can be separated into one of two groups by rules of origin: those that wholly originate or are obtained from one country and those goods whose production or manufacture involves materials or components from more than one country. Generally speaking, those exporting animals and animal products or plants and plant products are unlikely to find the rules difficult to apply, as these goods

EU market regulation affecting motor vehicles   35

will fall into the former category. Issues arise, however, in industries that traditionally rely upon a complex, integrated supply chain and typically function with high levels of imports and exports for the production of goods. The technology industry is one such example, with smart phone components being sourced globally, and the actual manufacture of the end product being performed in one or more countries that physically source few, or none, of the components. The automotive industry is another prominent example (Comments of Mr Mike Hawes, House of Lords, 2017).

Rules of origin and motor vehicle manufacturing

By virtue of the intra-EU free movement of goods, UK goods, when traded within internal borders do have to conform to any rule of origin (European Communities, 1976).[1] Post-Brexit, if a trade agreement is reached, in order to be afforded preferential treatment, exports from the UK will have to meet the rule of origin requirements as stipulated in that agreement. For example, in order to sell a car to Korea tariff-free under the EU-Korea trade deal, 'an EU car exporter must demonstrate that over 55% of the value of the car was created within the EU' as this is the standard stipulated within the EU-Republic of Korea Trade Agreement (Lowe, 2018).

Rules of origin are certain to apply to the UK vis-à-vis the EU after 29 March 2019, irrespective of whether the UK were to agree an FTA or was forced to operate under WTO rules. The only issue to be determined is which origin rules are applicable (House of Lords, 2017; para 131). If no agreement is reached, non-preferential rules of origin will apply under the WTO rules (World Customs Organization, 2018). If an agreement is reached, that agreement will determine the substance of the rules of origin for the relevant parties. Returning to the example of the EU-Korea FTA, the test of 'sufficient processing' is applied for the purposes of determining the nationality of goods (European Commission, 2011, p. 6).

Whilst not unique to the automotive industry, the rules of origin concept is of substantial concern for manufacturing and export viability. In order to fall within the purview of any preferential trade agreement that is likely to be reached, UK vehicle exporters will have to attest that their goods originate from the UK. Vehicles, the product of complex supply chains and comprised of components from a large number of countries, will likely struggle to meet a rule of origin requirement set at around 60% given that the value of the local content of UK-produced cars was around 40% in 2015. (A listing of EU preferential agreements is available at: European Commission, 2018a; see also Peter Wells; Automotive Council UK; Comments of Mr Mike Hawes; House of Lords, 2017.) Furthermore, when considering that currently imported components could not be easily substituted for domestic components the problem becomes doubly intractable.

Even if the level of local content issue can be overcome, there will be additional burdens. Any manufacturer seeking to export to the remaining EU countries post-Brexit will have to prove that the goods originated from the UK. This will generate a new administrative burden on manufacturers that previously had no need to attest the origin of their products for the purposes of accessing the EU market as, of course, they were already inside the EU. Though this is a notoriously difficult cost to calculate, estimates tend to range "between two and six per cent of product's final value" (Lowe, 2018, p. 2). This is a problem common to all UK industries, but is potentially more harmful to an industry that relies on fluid and responsive supply chains with 'just-in-time' and 'just-in-sequence' delivery and production (ACEA, 2018).

In addition, as the UK has been trading with third countries under the EU negotiated FTAs, UK vehicle manufactures benefit from an understanding of 'origin' as encompassing the EU. As a substantial proportion of the components used in UK manufacturing are from the EU and the EU will no longer be part of the same market, these components will, after 29 March 2019, be determined as non-native origin, decreasing further the ability of the vehicle industry to meet rules of origin for the purposes of preferential trade agreements.

In sum, supposing a comprehensive FTA with the EU is achieved and assuming that the benefits in the reduction of tariffs could potentially exceed the administrative burden of preferential rules of origin, the UK automotive industry may still simply be unable to comply with the domestic content requirements imposed by the EU's preferential rules of origin. The result would be a reversion to the WTO most favoured nation tariffs, causing substantial cost to UK exporters.

Achieving vehicle technical harmonisation

There are two methods by which the EU seeks to achieve technical harmonisation of vehicles: the creation of the EU-specific 'Whole Vehicle Type Approval System' (WVTA) and participation in the worldwide international harmonisation conducted under the auspices of the United Nations Economic Commission for Europe (UNECE).

Directives are the primary tool for setting EU standards. The original vehicle emissions applicable in what was then the European

Economic Community and its common market were set in Directive 70/220/EEC. These standards are sometimes now referred to as 'pre-Euro' and measured carbon monoxide and hydrocarbons for vehicles of different weight classes in three tests – cold start, idling and crankcase emissions. The directive recognised that "technical requirements must be rapidly adapted to take account of technical progress" and this directive remained in force for many years with amendments progressively tightening the applicable emissions standards.

The first set of contemporary standards, labelled Euro 1, was introduced in 1992 a full 22 years after the initial directive.[2] The Euro 1 standards led to the use of unleaded petrol and required cars to have catalytic convertors to achieve compliance (Automobile Association, 2017). Direct comparisons to the 1970 standards are problematic as the measurement categories differed, but since the introduction of Euro 1, a comparison to the current Euro 6 standards is illustrative of the successive tightening of emission requirements. Permitted emissions of carbon monoxide have been reduced by 63% while hydrocarbon emissions have been forced down by 83%. Despite the lengthy lag between the initial standards and the introduction of Euro 1, successive iterations of the regulations up to Euro 6 have been introduced on average every four and a half years. It is anticipated that Euro 7 will come into force sometime in 2020 with even more stringent controls (Frost & Sullivan, 2016).

Council Directive 70/156/EEC of 6 February 1970 sought to remove hindrances to the free movement of goods by establishing a community level type-approval procedure for vehicles. This framework did not itself stipulate the technical standards by which certificates could be issued but provided for the procedure whereby technical requirements could be stipulated by the separate directives. As such, over the years, 70/156/EEC was subject to a large number of amendments and addenda. One such, for example, was Directive 92/53/EEC, which limited application of the WVTA procedure to a specific vehicle category.[3] This process, over time, rendered Council Directive 70/156/EEC increasingly complex, unruly and lacking in clarity.

In response to this, and mindful of the need to make further alterations to Council Directive 70/156/EEC, Directive 2007/46/EC subsequently sought to 'recast' the provision for the WVTA system. Directive 2007/46/EC sets out the safety and environmental requirements that motor vehicles today have to comply with before being placed on the EU market. The directive makes the EU-WVTA system mandatory for all categories of motor vehicles and their trailers. A large number of UNECE regulations are also made mandatory. These replaced 38 directives previously in force.

38　*EU market regulation affecting motor vehicles*

Directive 2007/46/EC Article 49 repealed the 1970 Directive as amended,[4] and a new, streamlined system was implemented that broadly mimicked the approach of its predecessor. Under this new system, the applicable technical regulations were to be harmonised and specified as 'regulatory acts' listed in Annex IV of that directive. Of particular note for present purposes is the inclusion in Directive 2007/46/EC of UNECE regulations created under the 1958 UN agreement, with Article 3(1) defining a regulatory act as "a separate directive or regulation or a UNECE regulation annexed to the revised 1958 Agreement".

In this way, with a view to completing the internal market and to ensuring that it 'functions properly' (European Union, 2007; para 4), Directive 2007/46/EC sought to augment the scope and clarify the content of the by-now discarded Directive 70/156/EEC, so that all categories of vehicles fell within its purview. Pursuant to this, 2007/46/EC established a:

> harmonised framework containing the administrative provisions and general technical requirements for approval of all new vehicles within its scope and of the systems, components and separate technical units intended for those vehicles, with a view to facilitating their registration, sale and entry into service within the Community.
>
> (European Parliament, 2018)

This was the state of affairs until recently. In 2013, the Commission carried out an assessment of the EU legal framework for the type-approval of motor vehicles, which showed that the framework established by Directive 2007/46/EC is broadly "appropriate for achieving the main goals of harmonisation, effective functioning of the internal market and fair competition, and concluded that it should therefore continue to apply" (European Parliament, 2018). The assessment also noted, however, a number of inadequacies of the system (European Parliament, 2018; preambular para 4) that revealed a need for a 'fundamental revision' (European Parliament, 2018; preambular para 5). This has been recently effected by a major overhaul of the type-approval framework under Regulation (EU) 2018/858. The revised Regulation will make vehicle testing more independent, following the well-publicised scandals of emissions levels being reported. It will also lead to increased checks for vehicles in the EU market and to strengthening the system of European level oversight of emissions standards. The provisions therein become mandatory for all new vehicles from 1 September 2020 (by Article 91 of the Regulation), and Directive 2007/46/EC is then repealed at the same date (by Article 88 of the Regulation), with the first implementing steps to be adopted by the Commission no later than 5 July 2020. From this date, national authorities are prohibited from refusing EU type-approval for compliant vehicles (Article 91 of the Regulation).

Technological innovation has self-evidently accompanied tighter emission standards, and the legislation has induced technological change that the market alone is unlikely to have generated. Innovations that have accompanied the increasing Euro requirements include variable valve timing, direct fuel injection and highly sophisticated engine management systems (Auto Association Developments Limited, 2018). To ensure that the enhanced requirements are met, the EU also introduced new measurement procedures. The World-Harmonised Light-duty Vehicle Test Procedure (WLTP) measures CO_2 emissions and fuel consumption from cars and vans. The WLTP is intended to be a global measure and was developed together with the UNECE. In addition, to improve the understanding of vehicle performance in the 'real world', a Real Driving Emissions (RDE) test is being introduced to complement laboratory testing. These on-road tests will be performed in a combination of urban, rural and motorway driving and are to be fully employed by 2021 (Caudet, Von Hammerstein-Gesmold, & Noyon, 2018).

The European Commission oversees these vehicle standards and has a dual role. The Commission is led by 28 commissioners – one from each EU country (and is then about to have one less commissioner). Even though there is a commissioner from each EU country, the Commission is politically independent of the other EU institutions and the Member State governments. It represents and defends the interests of the EU as a whole, not their national positions. The Commission develops the legislative standards, including the emissions standards that will ultimately apply. It then also has an enforcement function ensuring these standards are applied.

The Commission, through its various committees, develops proposals for new legislation in many areas, not just vehicles, which is then 'adopted', that is, enacted, by the European Parliament and the Council of the EU (European Union, 2018). Specifically, the Working Group on Motor Vehicles (E01295) created in 1970 is devoted to discussions between stakeholders interested in regulatory activities concerning motor vehicles, and it assists the Commission in the preparation of legislative proposals (European Commission, 2018d). The importance of the legislative standards to the vehicle industry consequently leads

40 *EU market regulation affecting motor vehicles*

to many interested parties becoming involved in the discussions leading up to the implementation of a directive.

Vehicle safety in the EU has been regulated since 1958 in cooperation with the UNECE, which will be discussed in greater detail in the next chapter. Since the beginning, the driving force for these standards has been to remove barriers and increase trade between Member States and was led by the Inland Transport Committee's Working Party on the Construction of Vehicles based in Geneva. Initially, this committee developed a framework for voluntary type-approvals. In 1970 the EU implemented a new framework intended to be international in scope and led to the mandatory EU Whole Vehicle Type Approval (WVTA) process for cars. These requirements, however, only came into full effect in 1998 (European Commission, 2018e). Also in 1998, the EU became the voting representative in the UNECE for all Member Countries, and, as discussed below, drives the development of international standards. Numerous other countries subscribe to the UNECE standards, thus making them a near de facto global set of requirements. Today, the EU's work on safety is led through the European Commission's Directorate of Enterprise and Industry (European Commission, 2018e).

Upon leaving the EU, the UK will, of course, cease to be bound by the EUs WVTA. On 8 February 2018, in a *Notice to stakeholders* published through the Directorate-General for Internal Market, Industry, Entrepreneurship and SMEs, the European Commission addressed the repercussions of Brexit (European Commission, 2018b). The *Notice* details various consequences of the cessation of application of Directive 2007/46/EC – two of which are of primary concern for present purposes.[5]

The first is that manufacturers' representatives established in the UK will no longer be considered to be 'established in the EU', with the result that representatives will have to relocate or otherwise establish within the EU if they are to benefit from the WVTA. The second is that the UK approval authority will cease to be an EU approval authority, with the result that it will no longer be possible to place vehicles on the union market with no more than a certificate of conformity issued by the UK approval authority. Instead, manufacturers must seek certification from an EU approved authority (i.e. one of the remaining 27 Member Countries) (European Commission, 2018b).

It is difficult to imagine the first consequence being of any benefit to the UK. The presentation of the UK as a disadvantageous place of business was never an explicit part of the plan. The second consequence, however, does feed into the notion that Brexit will empower the UK to set its own standards. Whilst it is true that the UK approval authority will lose the power to issue certification for access to the EU marketplace, correspondingly, it will no longer be bound to accept European certification for entry to the UK marketplace. That this chimes with the oft espoused view that a vote to leave is a vote to take back control is not in doubt. But, independence from the certification process will be an illusory freedom, and, in any event, the utility of such an approach is questionable.

Notes

1 Goods not originally from the EU can be considered as originating in the EU where they have entered legally, by complying with the EU Common Customs Code and have had the necessary duties paid.
2 By convention, the versions of emission standards are labelled as Euro 1-Euro 6 (Arabic numerals) for light vehicles, and Euro I-Euro VI (Roman numerals) for heavy vehicles, however these usages are not always consistent in the literature. Since most of this text references light vehicles, primarily passenger cars, we use the Arabic numeral references.
3 Type M1: vehicles used for the carriage of passengers and comprising no more than eight seats in addition to the driver's seat.
4 Effective from 29 April 2009. Implicitly, Article 49 also repealed the Directives altering and amending 70/156/EEC.
5 Withdrawal of the United Kingdom and EU rules in the field of type-approval of motor vehicles. Available at: https://ec.europa.eu/info/sites/info/files/file_import/type_approvals.

References

ACEA. (2018). *Brexit: auto industry urges negotiators to avert worst-case scenario.* 17 November. Retrieved from https://www.acea.be/press-releases/article/brexit-auto-industry-urges-negotiators-to-avert-worst-case-scenario
Automobile Association. (2017). *Euro emission standards.* 11 December. Retrieved from https://www.theaa.com/driving-advice/fuels-environment/euro-emissions-standards
Auto Association Developments Limited. (2018). *Euro emission standards: limits to improve air quality and health.* Retrieved from https://www.theaa.com/driving-advice/fuels-environment/euro-emissions-standards
Caudet, L., Von Hammerstein-Gesmold, V., & Noyon, M. (2018). *Testing of emissions from cars.* European Commission Retrieved from http://europa.eu/rapid/press-release_MEMO-18-3646_en.htm
Coase, R. (1960). The problem of social cost. *The Journal of Law and Economics* (October). Retrieved from http://users.uom.gr/~esartz/teaching/envecon/coase.pdf
European Commission. (2011). *The EU-Korea Free Trade Agreement in practice.* Luxembourg: Publications Office of the European Union. Retrieved from https://publications.europa.eu/en/publication-detail/-/publication/4878c0b2-58be-4db9-8984-8982c8fb84b1

42 *EU market regulation affecting motor vehicles*

European Commission. (2018a). *Arrangements list*. Brussels. Retrieved from https://ec.europa.eu/taxation_customs/business/calculation-customs-duties/rules-origin/general-aspects-preferential-origin/arrangements-list_en

European Commission. (2018b). *Withdrawal of the United Kingdom and EU rules in the field of type approval of motor vehicles*. Brussels. Retrieved from https://ec.europa.eu/info/sites/info/files/file_import/type_approvals-automotive_vehicles_en.pdf

European Commission. (2018c). *How the Commission is organised*. European Commission. Retrieved from https://ec.europa.eu/info/about-european-commission/organisational-structure/how-commission-organised_en

European Commission. (2018d). *Register of Commission expert groups: Working Group on Motor Vehicles (E01295)*. European Commission. Retrieved from http://ec.europa.eu/transparency/regexpert/index.cfm?do=groupDetail.groupDetail&groupID=1295

European Commission. (2018e). *Who regulates vehicle safety?* Retrieved from https://ec.europa.eu/transport/road_safety/specialist/knowledge/vehicle/vehicle_safety_policy/who_regulates_vehicle_safety_en

European Communities, C. o. j. (1976). *Case 41/76 Donckerwolcke*. Retrieved from https://eur-lex.europa.eu/legal-content/EN/TXT/PDF/?uri=CELEX:61976CJ0041&from=EN

European Communities, C. o. j. (2006). *Commission v Greece*. Retrieved from http://curia.europa.eu/juris/liste.jsf?language=en&jur=C,T,F&num=65/05&td=ALL

European Union. (2007). *Directive 2007/46/EC of the European Parliament and of the Council: establishing a framework for the approval of motor vehicles and their trailers, and of systems, components and separate technical units intended for such vehicles*. Retrieved from https://eur-lex.europa.eu/legal-content/EN/TXT/PDF/?uri=CELEX:32007L0046&from=EN

European Union. (2012). *The treaty on the functioning of the European Union*. Geneva: Official Journal of the European Union. Retrieved from https://eur-lex.europa.eu/legal-content/EN/TXT/PDF/?uri=CELEX:12012E/TXT&from=EN

European Union. (2018). *European Commission: overview*. Retrieved from https://europa.eu/european-union/about-eu/institutions-bodies/european-commission_en

Frost & Sullivan. (2016). *European emission regulations – Will stringent emission regulations choke automotive industry or will OEMs find their way out?* 26 April. Retrieved from https://ww2.frost.com/frost-perspectives/european-emission-regulations-will-stringent-emission-regulations-choke-automotive-industry-or-will-oems-find-their-way-out/

HM Revenue & Customs. (2018). *Trading with the EU if there's no Brexit deal*. London. Retrieved from https://www.gov.uk/government/publications/trading-with-the-eu-if-theres-no-brexit-deal/trading-with-the-eu-if-theres-no-brexit-deal

EU market regulation affecting motor vehicles 43

Holmes, P., & Jacob, N. (2018). *Certificates and Rules of Origin: The Experience of UK Firms [UKTPO, University of Sussex, 2018]*. Retrieved from http://blogs.sussex.ac.uk/uktpo/files/2018/01/BP15-CRoO.pdf

House of Lords. (2017). *Brexit: trade in goods*. London: Published by the Authority of the House of Lords. Retrieved from https://publications.parliament.uk/pa/ld201617/ldselect/ldeucom/129/129.pdf

Lowe, S. (2018). *Brexit and rules of origin: why free trade agreements ≠ free trade*. 13 March. Retrieved from https://www.cer.eu/insights/brexit-and-rules-origin-why-free-trade-agreements-%E2%89%A0-free-trade

World Customs Organization. (2018). *Rules of origin – handbook*. Retrieved from http://www.wcoomd.org/en/topics/origin/overview/~/media/D6C8E98EE67B-472FA02B06BD2209DC99.ashx

WTO. (1994). *Agreement on rules of origin*. Retrieved from https://www.wto.org/english/docs_e/legal_e/22-roo_e.htm

WTO. (2019). *Technical information on rules of origin*. Retrieved from https://www.wto.org/english/tratop_e/roi_e/roi_info_e.htm

5 International standards

One of the broad arguments put forward by those advocating Brexit was that the UK can seek a less regulated approach, to industry and to society, with an implicit, or perhaps sometimes explicit, allegation that a big proportion of the unnecessary regulation emanated from the EU. Assuming Brexit happens – or perhaps we should put this as assuming Brexit will happen in the way envisaged by campaigners for leave – the UK will have the opportunity to define new approaches to car standards and enhancing environmental quality, which, as set out in the previous chapter, are the determining factors in vehicle product standards in EU Law. This chapter considers the optimum approach should the UK have the opportunity to operate independently of the EU. The argument however is that the independence from the EU will not mean independence from the market forces that underpin the industry or, perhaps to put this less prosaically, it will not mean independence from the international standards that will continue to apply whether or not the UK and the EU voices in this sector count as one.

The following chapter considers vehicle emissions in more detail. There are two methods by which the EU seeks to achieve technical harmonisation of vehicles: the creation of the EU-specific 'Whole Vehicle Type Approval System' (WVTA), and participation in the worldwide international harmonisation conducted under the auspices of the United Nations Economic Commission for Europe (UNECE). The first part of this chapter will address the WVTA, and the second will examine the UNECE. The chapter reviews the close relationship between EU and UN standards and notes how the adoption of UN standards is achieved. In concluding, this chapter will seek to appraise the current position and speculate as to the consequences for the UK car industry of leaving the EU, commenting on the proposition that the UK will be in an improved position once freed from EU regulation. The argument is that the UK's separation from the EU will not enable a separate voice at the UN decision-making table, because of the way in which UN standards are agreed.

UN standards

For present purposes, the relevant work of the UN in the regulation of vehicle standards is executed by the World Forum for Harmonization of Vehicle Regulations. This Forum, known as 'WP.29',[1] aims to develop new UN rules and harmonise existent rules in the areas of Active Safety, Passive Safety, Environmental Protection and General Safety. The work of WP.29 is governed by three Agreements. This chapter will detail the institutional position of WP.29 within the UN framework, before turning to the agreements and instruments through which WP.29 performs its duties.

Institutional position

The UNECE was formed in 1947 by resolution of the Economic and Social Council (ECOSOC) – a primary organ of the UN (ECOSOC, 1947). One of five regional commissions, the UNECE has 56 members, including, somewhat paradoxically, the United States of America, Canada and several Central Asian countries. The primary objective of the UNECE, as per the constitutive resolution, is to initiate

> measures for facilitating concerted action for the economic reconstruction of Europe, for raising the level of European economic activity, and for maintaining and strengthening the economic relations of the European countries, both among themselves and with other countries of the world.
>
> (ECOSOC, 1947)

Pursuant to this, the UNECE is tasked with 'making or sponsoring investigations and studies of economic and technological problems and developments' (ECOSOC, 1947).

In 1952, under the institutional framework of its Inland Transport Committee, which aspires to "improve competitiveness, safety, energy efficiency and security in the transport sector", the UNECE formed the World Forum for Harmonization of Vehicle Regulations known as WP.29 (United Nations, 2012).[2] WP.29 is itself sub-divided into various Groupes des Rapporteurs – each with an area of competence and expertise, such as Pollution and Energy as shown in Figure 5.1.

WP.29 aims to develop new UN Regulations, Global Technical Regulations (GTR) and UN Rules, in addition to harmonising, amending and updating existing UN Regulations, GTRs and UN Rules that address the areas of concern covered by the agreements it administers (United Nations, 2012). These legal instruments, the UNECE

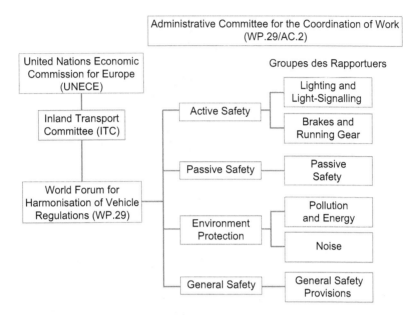

Figure 5.1 UN structure for vehicle regulations.
Source: United Nations, 2012, p. 10.

Agreements from which they emanate, and their significance to EU standards are detailed below.

Agreements and instruments

Three UN Agreements, adopted in 1958, 1997 and 1998, provide the international legal framework for contracting parties:[3]

- UN 1958 Agreement:[4] Concerning the Adoption of Uniform Technical Prescriptions for Wheeled Vehicles, Equipment and Parts which can be Fitted and/or be Used on Wheeled Vehicles and the Conditions for Reciprocal Recognition of Approvals Granted on the Basis of these Prescriptions;
- UN 1997 Agreement:[5] Concerning the Adoption of Uniform Conditions for Periodical Technical Inspections of Wheeled Vehicles and the Reciprocal Recognition of such Inspections;
- UN 1998 Agreement:[6] Concerning the Establishing of Global Technical Regulations (GTRs) for Wheeled Vehicles, Equipment and Parts which can be Fitted and/or be Used on Wheeled Vehicles.

International standards 47

The 1958 Agreement

Desiring to define uniform conditions that it will suffice for certain motor vehicle equipment and parts to fulfil in order to be approved in their countries, and desiring to facilitate the use in their countries of the equipment and parts thus approved by the competent authorities of another Contracting Party.
(United Nations, 2017a; preamble to original 1958 Agreement)

Originally only open for ratification or accession by UNECE member states, the present iteration of the Agreement currently has 53 parties of which 42 are UNECE members. Notably, for present purposes, both the UK and the EU are members (UNECE, 2019a, 2019c). The Agreement provides procedures for creating 'uniform prescriptions about new motor vehicles and motor vehicle equipment and for reciprocal acceptance of approvals issued' under 'UN Regulations' annexed to the Agreement (United Nations, 2012, p. 11). New UN Regulations can be adopted upon a four-fifths majority of those present and voting and will enter into force for all contracting parties 'which have not notified either their disagreement, or their intention not to apply it...'. This provision endows the regime with a relative suppleness, and UN Regulations 'have been adopted to varying degrees by the contracting parties'. It is worth noting that the EU, as a 'regional economic integration organization', is able to 'deliver the votes of its constituent sovereign countries' (United Nations, 2012, p. 47).

There are currently 145 such UN Regulations, which 'govern all categories of road vehicles and non-road mobile machinery and their equipment and parts' (United Nations, 2012, p. 11). The most recent concerns the 'uniform provisions concerning the approval of vehicles with regard to ISOFIX anchorage systems' (the international standard for attaching child safety seats) and entered into force on 19 July 2018 (UN Economic Commission for Europe, 2017).

The 1997 Agreement

This Agreement concerns the harmonisation of processes of technical inspections of vehicles and the acceptance of inspection documentation. There are twelve contracting countries including five smaller EU countries. Neither the UK, nor the EU as an organisation, belong. The narrow scope of the Agreement makes it of limited relevance for the present purposes.

48   *International standards*

The 1998 Agreement

> HAVING DECIDED that such process shall also promote the harmonization of existing technical regulations, recognizing the right of subnational, national and regional authorities to adopt and maintain technical regulations in the areas of health, safety, environmental protection, energy efficiency and anti-theft performance that are more stringent than those established at the global level.
>
> (ECOSOC, 2017, revision 3)

As the US and Canada follow a system of self-certification (UN Economic Commission for Europe, 2018a), these States found it difficult to implement the 'mutual recognition of approvals', as necessitated Article 3(2) of the 1958 Agreement, revision 3. By contrast, the 1998 'Global Agreement' invites participation from the world over and facilitates this by departing from the position of the 1958 Agreement in not requiring mutual recognition of approvals.

The 1998 Agreement complements the existing regime and has as a primary objective "[the reduction of] technical barriers to international trade through harmonizing existing technical regulations of contracting parties, and UN/ECE Regulations, and [development of] new Global Technical Regulations" (Economic Commission for Europe, 1998, p. 3). There are 38 contracting parties, including both the UK and the EU. In order to clarify its position regarding its member states, the EU entered a declaration upon ratification. This stated that it is "in matters within its competence that its Members States have transferred powers to it in fields covered by this Agreement, including the power to make binding decisions on them" (United Nations, 1998, p. 2).

In a similar relationship as established by the 1958 Agreement vis-à-vis UN Regulations, the 1998 Agreement utilises post-ratification annexed technical agreements to add substance to what is essentially a framework, or process-creating, treaty. Under the 1998 Agreement, GTRs play the functionally equivalent role of the UN Regulations.

A contracting party may tender a proposal to develop a GTR to an Administrative Committee for the Coordination of Work (United Nations, 2012, p. 28). If deemed permissible, and having been developed by the appropriate WP.29 Group des Rapporteurs, the Executive Committee may adopt the proposed text (UN Economic Commission for Europe, 2002, p. 4). A state, the representative of which voted in favour of adoption in the Executive Committee, is obliged to give effect to the GTR in its domestic law, unless a written explanation of a decision not to proceed is provided (United Nations, 2017b, p. 9).

GTRs cover a range of technical issues related to cars, motorcycles, three-wheeled vehicles, tractors and lorries. Individual GTRs include items such as testing procedures, on-board diagnostic equipment, glass safety glazing, head restraints, tyre testing and pedestrian safety. The first UN GTR, concerning 'door locks and door retention components', was adopted on 1 April 2005 (United Nations, 2004), and the 20th and most recent, concerning 'Electric Vehicle Safety (EVS)', was established on 14 March 2018 (United Nations, 2018). Because UN GTRs are not required to be adopted by the contracting parties, the impact of the 1998 Agreement on a post-Brexit UK is no different than it is in the current situation; UK export would need to abide by the regulations adopted by the individual importing country.

A summary of the structure of the three UN Agreements relative to vehicles is shown in Figure 5.2 below.

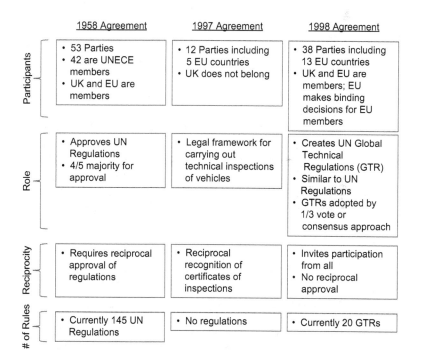

Figure 5.2 Summary of UN agreements related to vehicles.
Sources: 1958 agreement: https://treaties.un.org/doc/Treaties/1959/06/19590620%2009-15%20AM/Ch xi b 16.pdf; 1997 agreement: https://www.unece.org/trans/main/wp29/wp29wgs/wp29gen/wp291997.html; 1998 agreement: https://www.unece.org/fileadmin/DAM/trans/main/wp29/wp29wgs/; wp29gen/wp29glob/tran132.pdf.

50 *International standards*

UNECE voting procedures

An examination of the voting process in the UNECE will lay the groundwork for an elucidation of the UK's current (pre-Brexit) position and allow for a comparison with the supposed legal position post-Brexit. This will provide comment on the overarching question of whether leaving the EU will truly 'free' the UK from EU harmonisation of vehicle standards.

As noted previously, harmonisation of vehicle standards can be effected under the auspices of the UNECE via two legal Agreements, each yielding distinct yet only superficially different legal mechanisms. The primary differences being that the UN Regulations are, to some extent, replicated and absorbed by new UN Global Technical Regulations; the GTRs have a wider coverage, applying to both the US and Canada [7] and that there are far more UN Regulations (145) than GTRs (20).[8]

1958 Agreement (UN Regulations)

Under Revision 3, the most recent version of the Agreement, contracting parties vote through an administrative committee comprised of representatives of all parties, to adopt regulations (United Nations, 2017b; Article 1, p. 4; Appendix Article 5, p. 14). The EU, as a 'regional economic integration organization' votes with the number of their Member States being members of the UNECE (United Nations, 2017b; Article 6(1)). The appendix to the Agreement determines that a four-fifths majority of those voting is required to establish a draft as a UN Regulation (United Nations, 2017b, p. 14). The regulation will then be formally considered as adopted if, after a period of six months, not more than one-fifth of the contracting parties have notified the UN Secretary General of their disagreement (United Nations, 2017b, p. 5). As a result, a four-fifths majority must be maintained throughout, but after the initial vote the burden rests on opposition to show that there is sufficient (i.e. more than one-fifth) disagreement.

Amongst the 53 contracting parties are all 28 member states of the EU, plus the EU itself.[9] Hence, the EU represents all but 24 of the 53 contracting parties (not counting the EU itself). Post-Brexit, this will increase to 25. This level of participation means that the affirmative votes of 43 contracting parties are required to pass a regulation.[10] With the EU holding the votes of all of its 28 (soon to be 27) member states, it is not possible to pass a regulation without the acceptance or acquiescence of the EU and, if the EU wishes to propose and pass

International standards 51

a regulation, only another 15 (or 16 post-Brexit) votes are required to bolster the EU's considerable voting strength.

1998 Agreement (GTRs)

As with the 1958 Agreement, representatives of the contracting parties to the 1998 Agreement form an Executive Committee. This body has authority to review all recommendations and reports by working parties and has the ultimate determinative power on the establishment of new GTRs, in accordance with the formal requirements imposed by the Agreement (UN Economic Commission for Europe, 1998, pp. 4–5). The Agreement provides two distinct, but procedurally similar routes to the establishment of GTRs. The first applies to the harmonisation of existent standards, the second to the creation of standards on matters of which no prior internationally recognised standards exist.

The first route allows for standards to be listed in the 'Compendium of Global Regulations'. Standards can be entered into the compendium by a one-third vote of present and voting contracting parties (Economic Commission for Europe, 1998, pp. 5–6), provided that one-third includes the vote of the EU, Japan or the US. This is essentially an expedited procedure for those regulations (including the relatively copious UN Regulations) which have already attained a degree of international recognition and simultaneously provides a de facto veto for the large markets of the EU, Japan and US. The second route requires a consensus vote, essentially providing each contracting party with a veto (Economic Commission for Europe, 1998, p. 20).

Both routes result in the listing of the standard as a GTR. This however does not obligate each contracting party to adopt the standard within their domestic law; states maintain the ability to choose whether a standard is adopted, unless that state voted in favour of listing that standard as a GTR (Economic Commission for Europe, 1998, p. 11; Article 7(1)). This has the logical result that any GTR listed under the second route will ordinarily entail wholesale adoption. The exceptional cases of partial adoption being those where a contracting party exercises its right to notify the UN Secretary-General of a subsequent decision not to adopt the GTR (Economic Commission for Europe, 1998, p. 11; Article 7(3)). This provision gives force to the hortatory preambular recognition that it is ultimately the right of governments to determine whether the Global Technical Regulations "are suitable for their needs" (Economic Commission for Europe, 1998, p. 1).

It is also worth noting that in an attempt to stimulate high levels of treaty participation, the 1998 Agreement has flexibility in terms of

52 *International standards*

stringency (Economic Commission for Europe, 1998, p. 5). A developing state may choose to adopt a GTR with a lower level of stringency and aspire to achieve a higher level at a later date – though this has no application to UK adoption.

Having entered a declaration that member states have transferred their powers within the relevant field to the EU, and affirming the EU's ability to make binding decisions on its member states (Economic Commission for Europe, 1998, p. 13), the EU controls the votes of all its member states that are parties to the Agreement, but cannot also, simultaneously cast its own vote (Economic Commission for Europe, 1998, p. 19). There are currently 38 contracting parties to the 1998 Agreement, including 13 EU States,[11] the EU itself, and other economically powerful states such as the US, Russia, India, Japan, The Republic of Korea, India and China (UNECE, 2019b). Currently (i.e. prior to Brexit), the EU holds 13 votes, and post-Brexit the EU will hold 12 votes. As a result, if all contracting parties are present and voting, for the purposes of listing in the compendium, the EU will be one vote short of the one-third required. Whilst this is legally significant, it is of limited practical importance – of the 15 listings in the compendium only one has been proposed by the EU, with all others coming from the US (12) or Japan (2) (ECOSOC, 2018i, pp. 71–74).

Other participants

Finally, with respect to the role of non-contracting parties in negotiations, discussions and reports, a variety of relevant groups are welcome at WP.29 meetings. By virtue of Art. 2(3) of the 1998 Agreement, interested parties may be afforded consultative status and participate in the deliberative process where they have been granted consultative status by the United Nations Economic and Social Committee (ECOSOC), the UN agency in which all the examined apparatus is housed. For example, at a recent meeting of WP.29, a large variety of non-contracting party organisations with such ECOSOC status were present, including the Association for Emissions Control by Catalyst (AECC), Consumers International (CI), the European Association of Internal Combustion Engine Manufacturers (EUROMOT) and the European Tyre and Rim Technical Organization (ETRTO). (For a full list of participating contracting parties, see UN Economic Commission for Europe, 2018b, p. 6.)

Additionally, under Rule1(d) of the WP.29 Rules of Procedure, non-governmental organisations other than those possessing ECOSOC consultative status were in attendance (UN Economic Commission for Europe, 2018d, p. 4). These included the Recreation Vehicle Industry Association (RVIA) and the World Bicycle Industry Association (WBIA) (UN Economic Commission for Europe, 2018b, p. 6). All the mentioned organisations may participate in the deliberations but are not able to vote on any matters before the Administrative or Executive Committees.

The EU at the UNECE

The significance of the UN standards for the harmonisation inside and outside the EU is demonstrated by the consistent adoption of UN Regulations and GTRs, continual EU participation in UNECE processes, and by statements of commitment to the UNECE process made by various EU institutions and departments. In addition to the inclusion of UN Regulations as early as Directive 2007/46/EC, the reports of high-level groups indicate a considerable move towards both EU adoption of international harmonisation provisions and a clear intention to actively participate in, utilise and influence the international framework under the auspices of the UNECE.

Adoption of regulations

The EU acceded to the 1958 Agreement of the UNECE in 1998 (UNECE, 1997; Nb. Council Decision 2013/456/EU amended the decisions governing the 1958 Agreement after the Lisbon Treaty entered in force) and shortly after became a party to the 1998 Agreement (UNECE, 2000; Nb. Council Decision 2013/454/EU amended the Decisions governing the two Agreements after the Lisbon Treaty entered in force). An early indication of the intention to implement the provisions emanating from the UNECE framework can be gleaned from EU Directive 2007/46/EC of September 2007 which effected an overhaul of the pre-existing internal certification system of the EU. Article 3(1) of the directive defines a 'regulatory act' as 'a separate directive or regulation or a UNECE regulation annexed to the revised 1958 Agreement', with the result that even prior to accession to the UNECE 1958 Agreement the EU sought to implement standards via its own internal mechanisms. Of the provisions emanating from the two UNECE Agreements, the EU has adopted 129 of the 145 UN Regulations under the 1958 Agreement (ECOSOC, 2018b; Annex II, pp. 489–505), and 19 of the 20 GTRs under the 1998 Agreement (European Commission, 2019).

54 *International standards*

Participation in the process

In addition to participation in voting and adopting the majority of both UN Regulations and GTRs and voting in favour of every single GTR, and subsequent amendments (ECOSOC, 2018c, pp. 13–15), the EU also participates in the UNECE process by regularly sending commission representatives to the meetings of the various WP.29 Working Parties. In the last round of meetings, the European Commission was represented at the Working Party on Noise (ECOSOC, 2018f, p. 3), the Working Party on Lighting and Light-Signalling (ECOSOC, 2018e, p. 3), the Working Party on Pollution and Energy (ECOSOC, 2018h, p. 3), the Working Party on General Safety Provisions (ECOSOC, 2018d, p. 3), the Working Party on Passive Safety (ECOSOC, 2018g, p. 3), as well as the maiden session of the Working Party on Automated/Autonomous and Connected Vehicles (ECOSOC, 2018a, p. 1). Evidence that the EU is not merely a passive member of the UNECE is also demonstrated in its commitment to the UNECE Agreements by taking the leadership of the UNECE task force in charge of preparing the draft proposal to the 1958 Agreement (Buchmann, 2013).

Ongoing commitment

Pursuant to the EU's high-level group, CARS 2020 – established with the aim of reinforcing the automotive industry's competitiveness and sustainability – the European Commission has continually stated its ongoing commitment to the UNECE process, encompassing both the 1958 and 1998 Agreements (UNECE, 2014, p. 6). The CARS 2020 final report concluded by suggesting a variety of strategies for enhancing harmonisation standards globally in an attempt to curtail, reduce or eliminate barriers to trade. Notable for present purposes is the strong UNECE presence in the 'next steps', which included:

- Continuation of the work in the framework of the UNECE and by means of bilateral agreements with an aim of further international harmonisation of automotive legislation;
- Adopting the proposals for a reform of the 1958 Agreement and encouraging new countries to participate in the work under the UNECE framework; and
- Adoption by the WP.29 of the proposal for a new Regulation on IWVTA.

(Buchmann, 2013, p. 17)

International standards   55

A subsequent high-level group on competitiveness and sustainable growth of the automotive industry in the EU, GEAR 2030, was formally established by commission Decision C(2015) 6943 of 19 October 2015, and its findings are similar. The final report of GEAR 2030 likewise noted that in the face of increased competitiveness, the EU will need to respond in four broad ways, including, notably "[b]y co-operating internationally, most notably within the United Nations Economic Commission for Europe" (European Commission, 2017, p. 23).

In this way, it is clear that not only is the EU achieving a high degree of harmonisation with international standards through its adherence to UNECE standards, it is also an active participant and intends to continue its dominant role in international norm setting. This level of involvement shows the extent to which the EU is a committed rule-maker, not a passive rule-taker, and illustrates the utility of being on the inside looking out, rather than on the outside looking in.

Appraisal

The UK is, at the time of writing, expected to leave the EU. Resultantly, the UK participation in the EU Whole Vehicle Type-Approval System (WVTA) will cease altogether. With respect to participation and obligations emanating from the UNECE, the UK will (re)gain[12] its own vote as the EU's voting power is reduced to 27 (all member states post-Brexit), down from 28 votes. The UK will no longer be bound by the UN Regulations (from the 1958 Agreement) and GTRs (1998 Agreement) to which the EU has assented and will have to undergo the unusual process of readjusting its international obligations to fit with its pre-existing domestic regime.

> The UK will need to make a strong commitment that its regulatory standards will remain as high as the EU's. That commitment, in practice, will mean that UK and EU regulatory standards will remain substantially similar in the future.
>
> Many of these regulatory standards are themselves underpinned by international standards set by non-EU bodies of which we will remain a member – such as the UN Economic Commission for Europe, which sets vehicle safety standards.
>
> Theresa May, Mansion House Speech, 2 March 2018.
>
> (Prime Minister's Office, 2018)

This assessment of the UK's legal position vis-à-vis the EU with respect to the harmonisation of vehicle standards has been supported by the

56   *International standards*

pro-Brexit camp, chiming unerringly with the notion that leaving the EU increases freedom of action for the UK. This calculation is, however, narrowed-minded and short-sighted. It is true that the UK will have an independent veto under the 1998 Agreement for the purposes of creating new regulations (UN Economic Commission for Europe, 1998, p. 20), but the legal advantage of having an independent vote for other legal instruments, such as under the 1958 Agreement and listing of existent regulations under the 1998 Agreement, is minimal.

As Theresa May eluded to in the above extract, it is unlikely there will be a significant difference in the substance of the norms to be applied by the UK with respect to harmonisation of vehicle standards. May is correct to assert that leaving the EU, 'in practice', will not make any difference to domestic regulation in this area. It is not fair, however, to proclaim that the move can be seen as entirely neutral.

The EU, as has been detailed above, has a substantial share of the votes in the UNECE Agreements (both the 1958 and 1998), and has repeatedly, consistently and vigorously evinced a desire to continue with harmonisation through the mechanism of UNECE regulatory instruments. Resultantly, whilst achieving a fair degree of legal influence with respect to the 'first route' of the 1998 Agreement, the UK is set to lose influence within the de facto primary partner of the UNECE, namely, the EU.

Also of concern to the UK may be the listing of regulations in the compendium. This requires a one-third vote in the Executive Committee, with the affirmative vote of the EU, Japan or the US – these being the largest markets. The UK is now excluded from this beneficial position of influence.

Conclusion

The perception that the UK, by virtue of leaving the EU, can free itself from EU standards with respect to harmonisation of vehicles is correct in a myopic legal sense. Yet, it is unmeritorious in any meaningful, practical sense. Whilst the UK would indeed cease to be bound by EU standards, the proposals from GEAR 2030, the clear mutual desire for EU-UNECE uniformity, and EU participation in WP.29 negotiations and procedures are likely to ensure a high level of continuity between the two regimes, with the result that norms of identical content but disparate source would apply to the UK post-Brexit.

Though appearing to offer a rather neutral outcome, an understanding of the voting process reveals that whilst that the regulatory result of Brexit in this area may be minimal or even nil, the cost in terms of influence is substantial. May is correct in asserting that 'the UK and EU regulatory standards will remain substantially similar', but it would be disingenuous to suggest that those 'regulatory standards are themselves underpinned by international standards set by non-EU bodies'. From the above analysis, it is clear that the major player at the UNECE is the very union the UK intends to leave.

The UK will no longer have access to the European Parliament or Council, and no longer forms a part of a primary block within global car standards. The reality is that the loss of discreet, soft influence has been sacrificed for a superficial freedom which, the government has suggested, is unlikely to be used in any meaningful sense. In any event, given the greater market forces at work, this liberty is of dubious utility. With respect to car standards, the UK has gone from a position of subservience-in-name and relative power-in-reality, to the diametrically opposed position. Post-Brexit, the UK is free, but, most likely, only free to follow the EU-dominated UNECE process it was legally bound to follow pre-Brexit.

Notes

1 Not to be confused with 'Art.29 WP' – which was replaced by the European Data Protection Board by virtue of the EU General Data Protection Regulation (2016/679).
2 At the time of its formation, the Forum was named the 'Working Party of Experts on Technical Requirements of Vehicles.'
3 All of which are individual states, except the EU.
4 Registered 20 June 1959, entered into force 20 June 1959. Amended 10 November 1967, and revised 16 October 1995.
5 Registered 27 January 2001, entered into force 27 January 2001.
6 Accession 23 January 1998.
7 Owing to the issue of wholesale type approvals and self-certification, this was a primary objective of the 1998 Agreement. See: United Nations Publication, 'World Forum for Harmonisation of Vehicle Regulations (WP.29): How it Works', UN Doc. ECE/TRANS/NONE/2012/1, 2012, pp. 2, 25.
8 This is primarily due to the amount of time for which the Agreements have been in use, and given the process by which UN Regulations can be adopted under the 1998 Agreement, it is reasonable to expect the growth of GTRs to outpace that of the UN Regulations in the coming years.
9 Of the EU Member States, only Malta has not directly signaled its intentional to be a contracting party. However, Malta is bound by virtue of its accession to the EU on 1 May 2004. See: UN Treaty Series (United Nations, 1953).
10 The calculation is 42.4, which would be rounded up to 43 on the ordinary meaning of the terms of the Treaty. See Art31(1) Vienna Convention on the Law of Treaties 1969.

58   *International standards*

11 EU nations of Austria, Belgium, Bulgaria, Croatia, Czech Republic, Denmark, Estonia, Greece, Ireland, Latvia, Malta, Poland, Portugal, Slovenia and Slovakia are not contracting parties to the 1998 Agreement.
12 The UK acceded to the 1958 Agreement on 15 Jan 1963, but did not join the EU until 1 January 1973.

References

Buchmann, C. (2013). *Cars 2020: action plan for a competitive and sustainable automotive industry in Europe*. Brussels: European Union. Retrieved from https://www.google.com/search?q=european+commission+CARS+2020+-Action+Plan&rlz=1C5CHFA_enUS729US734&oq=european+commission+CARS+2020+Action+Plan&aqs=chrome..69i57.5751j0j7&sourceid=chrome&ie=UTF-8

Economic Commission for Europe. (1998). *1998 Agreement concerning the establishing of global technical regulations for wheeled vehicles, equipment and parts which can be fitted and/or be used on wheeled vehicles*. Geneva: United Nations. Retrieved from https://www.unece.org/fileadmin/DAM/trans/main/wp29/wp29wgs/wp29gen/wp29glob/tran132.pdf

ECOSOC. (1947). *Resolution 36 (IV) adopted by the Economic and Social Council during its Fourth Session from 28 February to 29 March 1947*. United Nations. Retrieved from https://treaties.un.org/doc/source/docs/NR075250.pdf

ECOSOC. (2017). *ECE/TRANS/WP.29/2016/2*. UN Economic and Social Committee. Retrieved from https://www.unece.org/fileadmin/DAM/trans/main/wp29/wp29regs/2017/E-ECE-TRANS-505-Rev.3e.pdf

ECOSOC. (2018a). *Authorization to develop a new UN GTR on Global Real Driving Emissions*. Geneva: United Nations. Retrieved from https://www.unece.org/fileadmin/DAM/trans/doc/2018/wp29/ECE-TRANS-WP29-AC3-51e.pdf

ECOSOC. (2018b). *ECE/TRANS/WP.29/343/Rev.26*. United Nations. Retrieved fromhttps://www.unece.org/fileadmin/DAM/trans/main/wp29/wp29regs/2018/ECE-TRANS-WP.29-343-Rev.26.pdf

ECOSOC. (2018c). *ECE/TRANS/WP.29/1073/Rev.23*. United Nations. Retrieved from https://www.unece.org/fileadmin/DAM/trans/doc/2018/wp29/ECE-TRANS-WP29-1073r23e.pdf

ECOSOC. (2018d). *Report of the Working Party on General Safety Provisions on its 115th session*. Geneva: United Nations. Retrieved from https://www.unece.org/fileadmin/DAM/trans/doc/2018/wp29grsg/ECE-TRANS-WP29-GRSG-94e.pdf

ECOSOC. (2018e). *-Report of the Working Party on Lighting and Light-Signalling on its eightieth session*. United Nations Retrieved from https://www.unece.org/fileadmin/DAM/trans/doc/2018/wp29gre/ECE-TRANS-WP29-GRE-80e.pdf

ECOSOC. (2018f). *Report of the Working Party on Noise on its sixty-eighth session*. United Nations. Retrieved from https://www.unece.org/fileadmin/DAM/trans/doc/2018/wp29grb/ECE-TRANS-WP29-GRB-66e.pdf

International standards   59

ECOSOC. (2018g). *Report of the Working Party on Passive Safety on its sixty-third session.* Geneva: United Nations. Retrieved from https://www.unece.org/fileadmin/DAM/trans/doc/2018/wp29grsp/ECE-TRANS-WP29-GRSP-63e.pdf

ECOSOC. (2018h). *Report of the Working Party on Pollution and Energy (GRPE) on its seventy-seventh session.* United Nations. Retrieved from https://www.unece.org/fileadmin/DAM/trans/doc/2018/wp29grpe/ECE-TRANS-WP29-GRPE-77a1e.pdf

ECOSOC. (2018i). *Status of the agreement, of the global registry and of the compendium of candidates, revision 23.* Geneva: United Nations. Retrieved from https://www.unece.org/fileadmin/DAM/trans/doc/2018/wp29/ECE-TRANS-WP29-1073r23e.pdf

European Commission. (2017). *Gear 2030: High Level Group on the Competitiveness and Sustainable Growth of the Automotive Industry in the European Union.* Retrieved from https://clepa.eu/wp-content/uploads/2017/10/GEAR-2030-Final-Report.pdf

European Commission. (2019). *Automotive industry – Global technical regulations.* Retrieved from http://ec.europa.eu/DocsRoom/documents/25343/attachments/1/translations/

Prime Minister's Office. (2018). *PM speech on our future economic partnership with the European Union.* London. Retrieved from https://www.gov.uk/government/speeches/pm-speech-on-our-future-economic-partnership-with-the-european-union

UNECE. (1997). *97/836/EC.* Retrieved from https://publications.europa.eu/en/publication-detail/-/publication/02a954fd-3b3b-4af3-bf82-f9682d820fed/language-en

UNECE. (2000). *2000/125/EC.* Official Journal of the European Communities. Retrieved from https://publications.europa.eu/en/publication-detail/-/publication/7214472a-d1df-46f8-8465-501045d22902/language-en

UNECE. (2014). *Progress report on the 2013 activities of the World Forum for Harmonisation of Vehicle Regulations.* Brussels: United Nations. Retrieved from file:///Users/douglasmunro/Downloads/swd-2014–178 en.pdf

UNECE. (2019a). *Member states and member states representatives.* United Nations. Retrieved from https://www.unece.org/oes/nutshell/member States representatives.html

UNECE. (2019b). *UN transport agreements and conventions: 1998 Agreement contracting parties.* Geneva. Retrieved from http://www.unece.org/trans/maps/un-transport-agreements-and-conventions-18.html

UNECE. (2019c). *UN transport agreements and conventions: contracting parties.* Geneva: United Nations. Retrieved from http://www.unece.org/trans/maps/un-transport-agreements-and-conventions-18.html

United Nations. (1953). *United Nations treaty collection: chapter XI transport and communications.* Geneva: United Nations. Retrieved from https://treaties.un.org/Pages/ViewDetails.aspx?src=IND&mtdsg no=XI-B-16&chapter=11&clang= en

60 *International standards*

United Nations. (1998). *Agreement concerning the establishing of global technical regulations for wheeled vehicles, equipment and parts which can be fitted and/or be used on wheeled vehicles.* Geneva. Retrieved from https://treaties. un.org/doc/Publication/MTDSG/Volume%20I/Chapter%20XI/XI-B-32. en.pdf

United Nations. (2004). *Global technical regulation No. 1: Door locks and door retention components.* Geneva. Retrieved from https://www.unece.org/fileadmin/ DAM/trans/main/wp29/wp29wgs/wp29gen/wp29registry/ECE-TRANS-180a1e.pdf

United Nations. (2012). *World forum for harmonization of vehicle regulations (WP.29): how it works.* New York and Geneva. Retrieved from http://www. unece.org/fileadmin/DAM/trans/main/wp29/wp29wgs/wp29gen/wp29pub/ WP29 Blue Book 2012 ENG.pdf

United Nations. (2017a). *1958 Agreement relating to vehicles.* Geneva. Retrieved from https://www.unece.org/fileadmin/DAM/trans/main/wp29/ wp29regs/2017/E-ECE-TRANS-505-Rev.3e.pdf

United Nations. (2017b). *1958 Agreement relating to vehicles, Revision 3.* Geneva. Retrieved from https://www.unece.org/fileadmin/DAM/trans/main/ wp29/wp29regs/2017/E-ECE-TRANS-505-Rev.3e.pdf

United Nations. (2018). *Global technical regulation No. 20: Global technical regulation on the electric vehicle safety (EVS).* United Nations. Retrieved from https://www.unece.org/fileadmin/DAM/trans/main/wp29/wp29wgs/ wp29gen/wp29registry/ECE-TRANS-180a20e.pdf

UN Economic Commission for Europe. (1998). *1998 Agreement concerning the establishment of global technical regulations for wheeled vehicles, equipment and parts which can be fitted and/or used on wheeled vehicles.* Geneva: United Nations. Retrieved from https://www.unece.org/fileadmin/DAM/ trans/main/wp29/wp29wgs/wp29gen/wp29glob/tran132.pdf

UN Economic Commission for Europe. (2002). *Guidelines regarding proposing and developing of global technical regulations.* Geneva: United Nations. Retrieved from https://www.unece.org/fileadmin/DAM/trans/main/wp29/ wp29wgs/wp29gen/wp29fdoc/800/TRANS-WP29-882e.pdf

UN Economic Commission for Europe. (2017). *Agreement Concerning the Adoption of Harmonized Technical United Nations Regulations for Wheeled Vehicles, Equipment and Parts which can be Fitted and/or be Used on Wheeled Vehicles and the Conditions for Reciprocal Recognition of Approvals Granted on the Basis of these United Nations Regulations.* Retrieved from https:// www.unece.org/fileadmin/DAM/trans/main/wp29/wp29regs/2017/E-ECE-TRANS-505-Rev.3e.pdf

UN Economic Commission for Europe. (2018a). *General questions related to WP.29 and its subsidiary bodies.* United Nations. Retrieved from http:// www.unece.org/trans/main/wp29/faq.html

UN Economic Commission for Europe. (2018b). *Reports of the World Forum for Harmonization of Vehicle Regulations on its 175th session.* Retrieved from https://www.unece.org/fileadmin/DAM/trans/doc/2018/wp29/ECE-TRANS-WP29-1139e.pdf

International standards 61

UN Economic Commission for Europe. (2018c). *Status of the agreement, of the annexed UN regulations and of amendments thereto: Revision 26*. Geneva: United Nations. Retrieved from https://www.unece.org/fileadmin/DAM/trans/main/wp29/wp29regs/2018/ECE-TRANS-WP.29-343-Rev.26.pdf

UN Economic Commission for Europe. (2018d). *Terms of reference and rules of procedure of the World Forum for Harmonization of Vehicle Regulations, Revision 1*. Geneva: United Nations. Retrieved from https://www.unece.org/fileadmin/DAM/trans/main/wp29/wp29wgs/wp29gen/wp29fdoc/600/ECE-TRANS-WP29-690rle.pdf

6　Vehicle emissions impact

The previous chapter analysed how the EU and UN standards apply as regulations to the car industry and discussed the scope for changes to these standards in a post-Brexit, 'take back control' world. This chapter focusses on the environmental triggers for so much of the regulation of car production. The stakes are high for the car industry, first because of the significant environmental impact from vehicle use, and second because of the publicity surrounding attempts to fool regulators as to the true emissions coming from new vehicles, specifically in the case involving Volkswagen (Hotten, 2015). The combination of 'dirty' and 'dishonest' is not an association the industry wants, and the branding of car manufacturers contrasts absolutely with it. Glossy brochures promoting 'green' innovation and cleanliness typify car products and new car showrooms are light and airy spaces.

This chapter furthers the argument that the UK will not have control in how it participates in the car industry and it does so by reference to vehicle emissions. It reviews the different types of pollutants caused by cars and the development of regulation to deal with pollutants in both Europe and the US. This review focusses on the measurement processes for pollutants and argues that the way regulators measure emissions will continue to limit the scope of the UK state's flexibility in agreeing separate trading arrangements when leaving the EU market. The uncertainty of the environmental challenge and the changes likely to how pollution standards are maintained will be an ongoing regulatory challenge.

Vehicles impact society in many ways; they are an integral part of the culture. A significant downside to the cultural prevalence of motor vehicles is the environmental impact of vehicle emissions. An extensive body of the rules applicable to vehicles relates to emissions standards and the acceptability of vehicles in markets other than those where they are made usually depends upon those vehicles' compliance with emissions standards. In order to understand how the car industry will operate in a post-Brexit environment, it is necessary to recognise how emissions are dealt with in the primary markets that shape the ability to trade. There are two broad categories of vehicle emissions: actual pollutants and greenhouse gas emissions. While both of these emission types can be considered pollution, they are dealt with differently from a legal standpoint.

Pollutants

The World Health Organisation (WHO) reports that 9 out of 10 people in the world breathe air with high levels of pollutants (World Health Organization, 2018). Emissions are the fourth leading risk factor for premature deaths worldwide and cost the global economy about US$225 billion in lost labour income in 2013 (World Bank, 2016). These are serious issues, but to investigate the vehicle industry relative to Brexit, it is useful to put the issue into context. The fact is that in some respects the environment is a success story: "In many parts of Europe, the local environment is arguably in as good a state today as it has been since the start of industrialization" (European Environment Agency, 2016b). Indeed, while the global situation remains poor, the fact is that more than 90% of deaths related to air pollution occur in lower income countries in Asia and Africa. There is little question that EU regulations related to pollution have benefitted the environment. And, these regulations have in turn impacted the motor industry.

The EU regulates five pollutant emissions under the National Emission Ceilings Directive:

- nitrogen oxides (NO_x)
- sulphur dioxide (SO_2)
- non-methane volatile organic compounds (NMVOC)
- ammonia (NH_3)
- particulate matter ($PM_{2.5}$)

(European Environment Agency, 2017)

Of these, NO_x and $PM_{2.5}$ are the two that importantly involve vehicles. The primary oxides of nitrogen are NO, nitrogen oxide, and NO_2, nitrogen dioxide. Each of these can harm the health of individuals, particularly those with respiratory illness. High and long-term exposure to these molecules can affect lung function and heighten the impact of allergens resulting in increased hospitalisation rates. Another impact of these oxides is the formation of smog and acid rain which can damage crops and contribute to ground-level ozone formation (Vehicle Certification Agency, 2018).

The various forms of particulate matter, commonly called soot, are emitted during the combustion of solid and liquid fuels, such as for power generation, domestic heating and in vehicle engines, particularly during the incomplete combustion of diesel fuel (Department for Environment Food and Rural Affairs, 2018). Soot can consist of hundreds of chemicals including sulphates, ammonium, nitrates and carcinogenic compounds such as arsenic, selenium, cadmium and zinc. These particulates are grouped in three categories: (1) coarse particulates which are less than 10 microns in diameter; (2) fine particulates which are less than 2.5 microns and (3) ultrafine particulates that are less than 0.1 micron in diameter. WHO estimates the death toll from inhaling these particulates is approximately 7 million people per year. These deaths result from conditions caused by breathing the particulates including stroke, heart disease, lung cancer, chronic obstructive pulmonary diseases and respiratory infections.

While these pollutants are serious, and need to be controlled, it must be recognised that under EU regulations levels of these pollutants related to vehicles have been declining. Nitrous oxide emissions in the UK fell from 1,139.5 Gg (or more understandably 1,139,500 tons) in 2010 to 918,300 tons in 2015, a decrease of more than 19% (European Environment Agency, 2017). Nearly two-thirds of that total were generated from two sources: energy production/distribution and road transport (i.e. vehicles). Figure 6.1 shows that these two primary causes have each declined over time, but the decrease from vehicles has been more uniform perhaps suggesting the retirement of older,

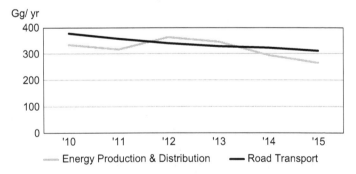

Figure 6.1 Annual UK Nitrous oxide output from energy production and road transport.

Source: European Environment Agency.

higher polluting, vehicles. A longer-term assessment of NO_x by the UK National Atmospheric Emissions Inventory indicates that this class of pollutants has declined by 71% since 1990 (BEIS, 2016).

For particulate matter one would gather from the media that diesel engines are the main culprit, and indeed in urban areas their impact is significant. However, in the UK there are three primary categories that contribute three-quarters of the $PM_{2.5}$: commercial, institutional and households, energy use in industry and road transport. It turns out that the major producer is commercial, institutional and households, which is more than the other two leading causes combined (European Environment Agency, 2017).

It also turns out that $PM_{2.5}$ output from road transport declined 26% between 2010 and 2015 in the UK versus an overall decline in the country of 7%. Figure 6.2 also shows that the performance of vehicles in the reduction of particulate matter has been more uniform than the other major categories which tend to move up and down.

It is also interesting to note that modelling by the UK Department for Environment, Food & Rural Affairs estimates that 20% of $PM_{2.5}$ pollution originates outside the UK and is transported by the wind to the country (Department for Environment Food and Rural Affairs, 2018). Much of that contaminate was likely generated by vehicle emissions but is out of the control of the UK motor industry or by domestic regulation.

Now, before turning to greenhouse gases, perhaps the greatest global concern for the environment, and another area where vehicles tend to shoulder much of the blame, it is worth noting that the situation could

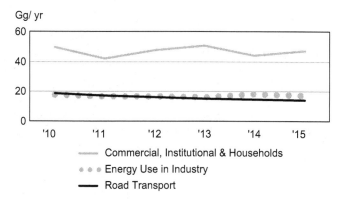

Figure 6.2 Annual UK particulate matter $PM_{2.5}$ output major sources.
Source: European Environment Agency.

66 *Vehicle emissions impact*

be far worse; actions taken by both the industry and the government have had an impact. According to the UK Department for Transport, "it would take 50 new cars to produce the same quantity of air pollutant emissions per kilometre as a vehicle made in 1970" (Vehicle Certification Agency, 2018). The pollution situation may not be great, but it is better than in the past.

Greenhouse gases

Greenhouse gases get their name from the fact that collectively they create an effect that helps trap some of the sun's radiation to warm the planet. Without that effect the world would be unliveable. However, when these gases are produced in excessive amounts the heat that is retained causes the planet to warm further which can have undesired consequences. Vehicles represent a major source of carbon emissions representing 14% of global greenhouse gas emissions and thus become another reason the vehicle industry attracts much environmental attention (EPA, 2018). Even though the production of vehicles is a relatively small portion of the overall economy, once produced they remain in service for years burning fossil fuels, so have a large cumulative impact on generated emissions (EPA, 2018). In 2015, transportation in the EU represented 23% of CO_2 emissions; in the US the share was 28% (EPA, 2018; Eurostat, 2017). It is estimated that about 40% of these totals occur in urban areas (Gately, Hutyra, & Wing, 2015). In addition, global emissions of CO_2 have continued to grow by 2.5% per year on average over the past decade which are at the high end of projected emissions scenarios (Friedlingstein et al., 2014).

The impact of greenhouse gas accumulation is a subject of much political debate, but according to the US National Institute of Environmental Health Sciences the consequences of climate change that leads to rising sea levels, more hurricanes, changes in shifting rainfall patterns and extreme heat waves all directly and indirectly impact the health of humans (NIEHS, 2018). The focus of this text is not to enumerate the impact of climate change, but to indicate how society will respond to the causes of these changes, and thus how the motor industry in the UK will be impacted post-Brexit. To this end, it is important to examine how society has attempted to deal with the question of the contribution vehicles make to pollution.

Clearly the growth of the vehicle population suggests that consumers have been willing to ignore, or at least rationalise, the environmental impact of their choices. For example, in the US, recent declines in fuel prices have driven the market towards larger, less fuel efficient and higher emission vehicle choices. In 2016, US sales of larger vehicles rose 7% while there was an 8% decline in the sales of small- and medium-sized cars (von Kaenel, 2017). The decline continued through 2018 with reduced sales of cars in general but increases in purchases of pickups, SUVs, vans and crossover vehicles (WSJ, 2018). The situation has actually led manufacturers to decide to drop production of a number of cars (Holley, 2018; Olsen, 2018; Snavely, 2017). The continuing growth in sales of larger vehicles contributes to a steady rise in greenhouse gas emissions. This shift to larger vehicles has been a market-driven outcome of lower fuel prices, despite a policy focus, at least until recently in the US, to reduce vehicle emissions and improve fuel economy. US consumers have repeatedly demonstrated a willingness to move to larger vehicles when petrol prices are down, regardless of the environmental consequences. As a result, society must confront how to deal with the issues.

Controlling pollutants: markets versus regulation

Political discourse is often carried out in extremes; the politics of pollution is no exception. Some environmentalists insist that forcing firms to eliminate pollution is the objective, while free market supporters argue that excessively broad regulations result in reduced productivity and higher costs. Part of the reason these arguments continue is that economic theory will not determine the best course of action, only identify choices and estimate the potential costs. The Nobel Prize winning economist Ronald Coase argued in a seminal 1960 article examining how to optimise the social choices facing society that "...the whole discussion is largely irrelevant for questions of economic policy since whatever we may have in mind as our ideal world, it is clear that we have not yet discovered how to get to it from where we are" (Coase, 1960). The fact is that economics is very bad at resolving normative issues about what is right and wrong or what should be done. If there is no societal consensus of what the issues are and what an appropriate outcome might be, it is unlikely that either the market or regulations will achieve results that gain widespread support.

Assuming, however, that there is some general agreement that the level of pollution is too high, and the accumulation of greenhouse gasses is excessive, then society is likely to take some action. Economists argue that policy decisions should be made at the margin – identifying the incremental benefits and costs of any particular action and adopting the solution that leads to the greatest social benefit. This approach does not require that an ideal outcome be identified, only that any particular

68 *Vehicle emissions impact*

action have benefits that exceed costs. The major problem for the real world is that these discussions and the subsequent decisions are always made in the face of imperfect information, and from an economic standpoint there are two broad and related complications in the analysis of environmental questions: externalities and the lack of property rights.

Externalities

Externalities are 'things' that occur which in theory should be taken into account in the decision process, such as the production of motor vehicles, but are not because they are unknown, difficult to measure or impractical to allocate. Externalities can be both positive and negative, and both cause resources to be distributed in a less than optimum manner, but in the case of the motor industry, most of the externalities tend to be negative; that is, they impose societal costs that are not considered by the industry in their manufacturing decisions. Indeed, if a motor vehicle manufacturer unilaterally decided that their products caused damage to the environment that should be paid for, voluntarily decided to raise prices to donate to environmental repair, and the competition did not follow, that firm would be punished in the marketplace by fewer sales, lower profits, falling stock price and a shareholder revolt. Thus, even if a firm recognises that their actions cause externalities, the marketplace can make it difficult to follow a 'socially responsible' path.

The negative externalities related to the vehicle industry and emissions are extensive. It is fairly straightforward to measure the emissions of vehicles, but it is a challenge to definitively measure the consequences of those emissions on people and property. To what extent do particulate emissions cause health problems, and what is the cost of curing those conditions? Health problems may well have multiple causes and determining the extent the vehicle industry is responsible is problematic. In addition, the vehicle industry is not the only polluting entity. How do their emissions combine with pollutants from other activities? The market will not be able to make effective decisions in the absence of complete information.

Property rights

Related to externalities, and complicating the decision process, is the issue of the lack of property rights in many situations. Property rights are important to efficient economic outcomes. Since no one individual or group owns the atmosphere, no single corporation will benefit from investing in eliminating its pollution, particularly if other firms continue to pollute, and thereby increase their profits. If someone actually owned the atmosphere, they would certainly act against anyone who harmed it. But given that the atmosphere is a public good, the market will not take it into account unless forced. That was essentially the reason behind the creation of the National Rivers Authority in 1989, now part of the Environment Agency of England and Whales. The idea was to give the agency the power to act as if it owned the country's rivers, and thus to behave in a way to force firms to treat these public assets with respect. However, many aspects of the earth are not privately owned, and thus subject to being ignored by firms.

Emphasising the above arguments, it is interesting to note that one of the winners of the 2018 Nobel Prize in Economics is William Nordhaus of Yale University. His work was the first to create quantitative models that explain the interaction between the climate and the economy. The research underscores the conclusion that markets left on their own will not achieve desirable outcomes for the environment.

While the marketplace by itself is unlikely to control carbon emissions because of imperfect information, externalities and lack of property rights, it can also be argued that regulation has not been effective as the above data on the extent of pollutants indicates. Regulatory efforts are combinations of idealism and political opportunism that can mitigate potential improvements in market performance. Tension between market efficiency and regulatory restraint is not new. The arguments on either side are often driven (particularly in current times) by the ends of political spectrums and limit dispassionate debate on alternatives. This manuscript cannot resolve the conflicting positions but is an attempt to stimulate discussion of the likely outcomes of choices that have been, and are yet to be, made.

Complicating the regulation versus market-driven approach to environmental quality is a rapidly changing technological setting and moves by larger metropolitan cities to tackle the problem head-on. Growth in hybrid powertrains, improvements in electric vehicles and the likely introduction of efficient driverless vehicles are factors currently outside the regulatory framework, but likely will be in the future. Beyond technology, recent efforts by London and Paris to establish their own standards for vehicles to both improve the environment and reduce congestion complicate the regulatory situation and will impact the production decisions of vehicle manufacturers. This aspect is considered in more detail in Chapter 9. As Brexit approaches, and the UK makes decisions to define a new regulatory environment, these dynamics will impact its ability to effectively do so. The question is: how to find an optimum approach?

70 *Vehicle emissions impact*

Brief history of the development of vehicle regulations

Given that the free market is unlikely to adequately account for the societal harm of pollution emitted by vehicles, concerned citizens will turn to the government. The development of government regulations is always a complex combination of need and politics. In the case of vehicle emissions regulations, the outcome also evolved alongside a broader set of requirements including safety and fuel economy. The landscape is complicated by separate requirements in multiple pieces of legislation, rule-setting by regulatory agencies and provisions set forth in trade agreements. As the UK sets out on an independent path which it intends to lead to greater opportunities for its trade and economy, it is useful to explore the different dynamics of the regulatory environment in Europe and the US to understand the constraints that the UK will face in its new future.

Europe

In the case of Europe, the history of emissions regulations traces its roots to work done by a subsidiary of the United Nations Economic Commission for Europe (UNECE) beginning in 1952. A Working party on the Construction of Vehicles developed a plan to "initiate and pursue actions aimed at the worldwide harmonization or development of technical regulations for vehicles" (UNECE, 2017). The result was a 1958 UN agreement relating to vehicle safety, environmental protection, fuel efficiency and anti-theft occurrence (United Nations, 1958). Signatories to the agreement accepted limited mutual recognition of approvals for vehicle components, but not complete vehicles.[1] The US did not sign the 1958 UNECE agreement because it was opposed to committing to standards developed by other countries. Thus, most US-made vehicles cannot be exported to many countries without modifications (Moguen-Toursel, 2007, p. 8).

Initially the development of EU vehicle regulations was not based on a high level of environmental protection. This is because the Treaty of Rome has no provision for environmental policy-making. Thus, the development of EU environmental regulations was fundamentally an outgrowth of efforts to remove internal barriers to trade, adopting Article 100 of the treaty which relates to the free movement of goods as a legal foundation (Stephen, 2000). Additional complications in implementing vehicle environmental controls resulted from the differential composition of the manufacturing base in the major markets. For example, Italy placed high taxes on large displacement engines, the UK favoured "company" cars which focused on mid-sized powertrains, while the absence of speed limits on German autobahns led to production of larger displacement engines. Engine size impacts both the form and cost of environmental regulations, and thus resulted in lengthy political negotiations leaving each state to act alone (Stephen, 2000).

Consequently, prior to the mid-1980s it was common for EU member countries to adopt some UNECE produced regulations relating to safety, environmental protection and energy efficiency; however each country modified the standards as it saw fit. In 1985 the member States signed the Single European Act (SEA) with a goal of unifying the European market. Under this act automobile emissions regulations were harmonised across Europe in 1987 although the SEA allowed member States to maintain more stringent measures, and this flexibility within harmonised standards has broadly remained in place. Vehicle exhaust regulations were implemented in 1970 although the first EU-wide standard, called Euro 1, was only introduced in 1992 (RAC, 2017). The current standards, Euro 6, control emissions of nitrogen oxides, carbon monoxide, hydrocarbons and particulate matter. The impact has been dramatic. It is estimated that adoption of Euro 6 emission standards will reduce the emission of fine particulate matter by up to 99% and reduce the risk of heart disease, lung cancer, stroke and asthma (Williams & Minjares, 2016).

The EU does not set fuel economy standards for vehicles directly as is the case in the US. Instead, the EU sets standards for greenhouse gas emissions, and through these regulations fuel economy can be estimated. The first of these standards was implemented in 1998–1999 as a voluntary cooperation between the European Commission (EC) and automotive manufacturers. However, the industry failed to meet the voluntary average fleet requirements, and as a consequence the EC developed mandatory targets in 2009. The regulation established CO_2 emission targets to be achieved progressively by 2015 and 2020 (European Parliament, 2009).

In tandem with emissions regulations, it can also be argued that the EU member states adopted a market approach to increasing fuel economy by imposing high fuel taxes. Figure 6.3 below shows the tax per litre of petrol in Euros for the countries that represent 75% of the 2016 EU market for new vehicle sales contrasted with the US tax.

It can be argued that these taxes are an attempt to cover the negative externalities of petrol use, thus providing a more accurate market value for the cost of fuel. Overall, the current EU average petrol tax is €0.68/litre, which is more than six times the level in the US. These taxes certainly drive customers towards smaller vehicles which increases fuel economy, and as a side benefit reduces emissions.

72 *Vehicle emissions impact*

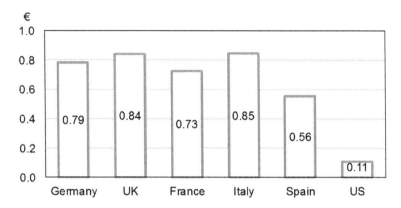

Figure 6.3 Petrol tax (€/litre) in EU countries representing 75% of the 2016 Car Market versus the US.
Source: US Department of Energy

United States

The history of US vehicle regulations follows a path that is similar to other regulatory processes in the states – policy significantly intertwined with politics. In the early decades of the automobile, regulation was virtually non-existent. A study of the industry at that time indicated that "Regulating...vehicle design at the national level did not conform to existing political ideas about the appropriate federal division of responsibilities or... the federal government's constitutional power to regulate interstate commerce" (Mashaw & Harfst, 1990, pp. 30–31). Individual states determined the guidelines that prevailed in their jurisdiction, although these rules were often based on Society of Automotive Engineers (SAE) guidelines. Initial steps at uniformity were taken in 1926 when a voluntary Uniform Vehicle Code was created to replace the many different state rules. The guidelines specified the types of lighting, reflectors, brakes, mirrors and tyres that cars should have. While widely accepted, by 1946 only 30 of the 48 states had formally adopted the code (Davis, 1963).

Rising US vehicle deaths in the 1950–1960s caused by increasing vehicle traffic, particularly with the creation of the interstate highway system, led to a public uproar and congress was pushed to finally implement national policy. The National Traffic and Motor Vehicle Safety Act of 1966 consisted of two parts. The first mandated that each state put in place a highway safety programme in accordance with federal standards to improve driver performance, accident records and traffic control; the second created safety standards for all motor vehicles.[2]

The US approach to emissions standards followed a similar pattern of federal reluctance. California was the first state to address emissions resulting in high levels of pollution. In 1947, Los Angeles banned the use of coal and fuel oils for industrial purposes. Research at the California Institute of Technology demonstrated that nitrogen oxides and hydrocarbons exposed to sunlight caused eye and throat irritation and reduced visibility. Further studies connected the problems to engine exhaust. Thus, California became the first state to establish air quality standards and controls for motor vehicle emissions in 1959 (Melosi, 2004). This finally led the US Congress to act, based on the concern that different regulations created by individual states would be detrimental to the vehicle industry. The initial step by the federal government to address air pollution came in 1955 with the Federal Air Pollution Control Act, but only provided funding to state and local governments to address the problem. California continued to lead the regulatory process with additional emissions regulations in 1961, 1964 and 1968. The federal government continued to lag California with the first national legislation to actually control air pollution only coming with the Clean Air Act of 1963. Further catch-up amendments to the law were enacted in 1965, 1967 and 1970. Since then environmental pressures have led to greater public discussion, although every attempt to increase regulation is resisted strongly by entrenched economic interests.

Fuel economy standards in the US were also non-existent until driven by external forces. The oil embargo of 1973 imposed by the Organization of the Petroleum Exporting Countries (OPEC) led to the passage of the Energy Policy and Conservation Act which established Corporate Average Fuel Economy (CAFE) standards for new passenger vehicles. The impact was substantial. Between 1975 and 1988, the average fuel economy of new automobiles increased 81%, from 15.8 to 28.6 mpg (Canis & Lattanzio, 2014). The recognition that fuel economy was tied to greenhouse gas emissions led to subsequent requirements, culminating in a 2009 agreement with the Obama administration to tie light duty vehicle fuel efficiency standards to greenhouse gas (GHG) emission standards with significant increases required by 2025. However, as will be detailed later, these requirements are being challenged by the Trump administration which in March 2017 ordered a review of the requirements and installed an environmental sceptic as head of the Environmental Protection Agency (Eisenstein, March 16, 2017).

Emissions – measurement process and environmental concerns

The government Brexit White Paper indicates a willingness to accede to the European testing regime for emissions (UK Parliament,

74 *Vehicle emissions impact*

2018, p. 21). However, since one of the prime motives behind Brexit is to achieve the ability to operate independently it is necessary to understand the differences between the major measurement schemes to determine how an independent course might need to operate. The processes in Europe and the US are significantly different, even though they are pursuing similar measurements. The methods themselves drive regulatory conditions that will impact the ability of the UK to assert an independent approach.

Europe

Traditionally, measures of vehicle emissions in Europe are carried out in a laboratory, with vehicles tested on a dynamometer under strictly controlled conditions to ensure consistency across models and repeated tests. The test regime is called the New European Driving Cycle (NEDC). In addition to the dynamometer analysis, the NEDC process involves a test outside the laboratory where a vehicle is allowed to coast from a specified speed, with the engine idling, until it stops. The testing process in Europe was not actually intended to represent the 'real world'. When the NEDC test was introduced in 1970 it was meant to measure the achievement of tightened emissions standards. What was wanted was a reproducible test procedure. Fuel consumption was a by-product of the measure, and expected to be used only for consumer information as there was no regulatory requirement for fuel economy (Mock et al., 2013). However, in 2007–2008 several EU countries introduced vehicle taxation systems based on CO_2 emissions and a mandatory EU CO_2 regulation for new cars was introduced. This has led to an increased desire for data that more accurately represent actual vehicle usage.

As might be expected determining 'real-world' performance encounters measurement challenges. These include differences in vehicles (e.g. levels of equipment), driver performance variations and dissimilarities in vehicle use. For example, Travelcard[3] data in the Netherlands demonstrated that fuel consumption for a specific model of vehicle can vary from 70 to 180% of the calculated type-approval value (Mock et al., 2013). A separate Netherlands study showed that loads carried by vehicles driven in realistic conditions are considerably higher than the loads used in the testing process. These differences ranged from 30% at high speed to 70% at low speeds (Kadijk & Ligterink, 2012). Compounding the discrepancy of laboratory versus use data, testing procedures allow manufacturers some flexibilities that can enhance

Vehicle emissions impact 75

their measured results compared with on road performance. For example, the legislation allows:

- Flexibility in the choice of wheels, tyres and tread depth that can improve rolling and aerodynamic resistance
- Flexibility in tyre pressure based on setting the temperature for a 'cold' start
- Adjustments in brakes to eliminate losses from unintentional braking
- Some ability to optimise vehicle temperature during testing
- Modifying the out-of-lab test road surface to lower rolling resistance

Within the test itself, there are flexibilities that allow manufacturers to:

- Reduce the weight of vehicles by specifying certain items to be classified as dealer installed options
- Adjust tolerances of laboratory instruments to one end of the allowable range
- Adjust the temperature in the test cell
- Use standard 'table values' for testing vehicles that have relatively high aerodynamic or rolling resistance
- Modify the gear shift schedule for some vehicles

Beyond these flexibilities there are factors in the test process itself that impact outcomes compared with the 'real world'. During the test, all systems (e.g. heated seats, window defrosters, air-conditioning and entertainment systems) are turned off. In addition, cargo options such as roof racks and rear cargo boxes that could impact resistance are removed (European Environment Agency, 2016a, p. 37). All of these adjustments are completely legal, and in part intended to enable testing repeatability, but they have the consequence of deviating from 'real world' conditions. It is also likely that increasing regulatory pressure and consumer attention encourage manufacturers to pay more attention to testing outcomes than was the case in the early years of the scheme. As a result, values of various laboratory results compared with on-road experience have widened. For example, CO_2 emission differences between laboratory and on-road tests differed by less than 10% in 2001, but by 2011 had risen to approximately 25% (Mock et al., 2013).

76 *Vehicle emissions impact*

The recognised weaknesses of the NEDC process have led to efforts to develop a more realistic testing approach. The UN began work on a 'World-Harmonized Light-duty Vehicle Test Procedure' (WLTP) in 2008. The procedure that was created contains a test cycle that is more representative of normal driving behaviour, and also limits allowed loopholes. The European Commission is working on implementing the WLTP although timing has yet to be agreed. Compared with the current NEDC, the expectation is that the WLTP will increase the measured output of CO_2 by 6–8% depending on the testing temperature (Mock et al., October, 2014). In addition to the CO_2 test procedure the EU has agreed a Real Driving Emission (RDE) test procedure for cars and vans. When introduced, the EU will be the first in the world to use on-road emissions testing methods for legal compliance purposes (European Environment Agency, 2016a, p. 50). The new RDE procedure will measure emissions of NO_X using Portable Emission Measuring Systems (PEMS) attached to the car. The new regulations will require that actual driving emissions be less than the legal limits adjusted by a 'conformity factor' that will be set by regulators. Those rules remain subject to governmental approval. It is hoped that the outcome will be greater alignment between laboratory measures and 'real world' experience to raise consumer confidence in the measurement process. However, it needs to be noted that the on-road testing in Europe will still be performed by manufacturers with many of the modifications to improve results in the laboratory allowed (Hakim & Mouawad, 8 November, 2015).

United States

Comparing vehicle greenhouse gas and/or fuel economy standards between Europe and the US is difficult because the standards differ greatly in structure and testing methods. Differences between the two include distance, duration, vehicle speed and cold start (Canis & Lattanzio, 2014). In the US there is less flexibility in the testing procedure than in Europe and methods used for regulatory purposes are highly standardised. Emission regulations have detailed descriptions of the measurement process including the setup, the type of equipment to use and the procedures to be followed (Majewski & Burtscher, 2011). Manufacturers test one representative vehicle from each combination of vehicle by weight class, transmission group and engine. Tested vehicles are put through a series of test cycles that specify vehicle speed for each point in time during the laboratory tests. Vehicles are put through tests designed to represent city and highway driving as well as tests to

Vehicle emissions impact 77

account for (1) faster speeds and acceleration, (2) air conditioner use and (3) colder outside temperatures (US Department of Energy, 2017). All of these tests are conducted in a laboratory environment, although the EPA is beginning to conduct on-road tests using a PEMS system.

The rigid specification of the testing procedure is a double-edged sword. Manufacturers have long known the exact test conditions the EPA uses to measure vehicle emissions. The level of specification allowed Volkswagen to design its engine management software explicitly to detect when a vehicle was being tested, which would then send the engine into a mode to pass the test (Sorokanich, 9 November, 2015). VW is the only manufacturer to have pleaded guilty to this type of evasion, however the US government filed suit against Chrysler alleging a similar type of evasion, and in January 2019 the firm, without admitting guilt, agreed to pay a fine of more than £600 million. Criminal investigations in the case remain ongoing. On a per car basis the Fiat Chrysler fine was greater than that assessed to VW because, as the acting Environmental Protection Agency administrator stated: "...they kept reassuring us that they were not cheating" (Beene, Mehrotra, & Coppola, 2019; Krisher, 2017).[4]

In the wake of the VW case, US regulators have decided to expand on-road testing. The EPA is selecting random vehicles to put through tests that are not being publicised. Manufacturers have asked the EPA to explain the new test conditions, but have been told they have no need to know (Hakim & Mouawad, 8 November, 2015). However, US regulators are not convinced that on-road tests are sufficiently robust to be used for regulatory purposes, so for the foreseeable future the on-road tests are for verification purposes only. The upshot of the new, 'real-world', emissions test is that the processes in Europe and the US are diverging further (Hakim & Mouawad, 8 November, 2015).

Beyond these procedures, the EPA conducts a large public system for measuring fuel economy standards, called My MPG, the programme allows individuals to register a vehicle and report their fuel economy experience. Those who do not care to participate are still able to view the data by car model which enables consumers to compare results versus the laboratory data that are printed on the vehicle's price sticker (Office of Transportation and Air Quality, 2017).

Current regulatory challenges

The US regulatory system, particularly the fuel economy standards, is under attack by the Trump administration and may well be rolled back. As part of the March 2017 announcement ordering a review

78 *Vehicle emissions impact*

of the fuel economy requirements, the administration announced that every federal agency would set up a task force to identify and remove "any regulation that undermines American auto production" (Carey & Shepardson, 15 March, 2017). In August 2018 the Trump administration proposed that the fuel economy increases implemented by the Obama administration as part of the agreement for federal bailouts during the financial crisis be overturned. Those requirements, agreed in 2012, nearly doubled the CAFE standards for cars and light trucks by 2025. Ironically, at the time of implementation, the 2012 regulations were hailed as an effective collaboration between industry, government and environmentalists. Car makers got regulatory certainty, consumers would have savings from fuel consumption and the carbon footprint of the transportation sector would shrink (Sperling, 2018). A survey conducted by the Pew research organisation included laudatory statements by BMW, Honda, General Motors, the National Association of Manufacturers and the United Auto Workers labour union (Pew Environment Group, 2011).

The Trump administration intends to maintain laxer 2020 standards through to 2026. Their argument for the change (other than it is another way to reverse anything from the Obama years) is that the rollback will lower vehicle prices which in turn will induce more vehicle sales. This, they argue, will lead to a reduction in societal costs from fewer fatalities, injuries and damage because older vehicles are less safe (US Department of Transportation, 2018). Multiple outside analyses challenge the administration's assertions as inconsistent with established facts, not to mention the complete omission of the savings from less oil use both for consumers and the environment. Perhaps most importantly from the standpoint of how the UK would deal with the US in this industry post-Brexit is the fact that the proposed regulatory change has led to legal challenges which are likely to result in uncertainty for years (Sperling, 2018). The overall outcome is that the degree of vehicle regulation in the US is likely to change, also moving Europe and the US farther apart.

Brexit consequences

From the standpoint of the motor vehicle industry in the UK, a post-Brexit environment characterised more by significant uncertainty will necessarily force hard decisions on the part of UK manufacturers as to how and to what degree they can choose to try to increase trade with the US. The UK will be free to implement their own regulations, but that will have little impact unless those changes match the US

Vehicle emissions impact 79

requirements which are going to be uncertain for some time. The same will be true for relationships with the EU; freedom of choice is of little value if the international environmental rules dictate the terms. Environmental requirements, particularly for vehicles, highlight the dichotomy that exists between the hope of Brexit for autonomy and the necessity of international cooperation for the environment.

Notes

1 All signatories were European countries until 1995 when the agreement was changed to allow non-UNECE members. http://www.unece.org/trans/main/wp29/faq.html.
2 The importance of the book _Unsafe at any speed: the designed-in dangers of the American automobile_ by Ralph Nader should also be noted. This book highlighted the lack of safety items in vehicles and led to pressure on the federal government to act. It has also been argued, however, that the federal regulations raised vehicle costs and reduced performance in the 1970s compared to European vehicles and began the decline of US vehicle dominance.
3 Travelcard is a system in the Netherlands that can be used to pay for fuel. It is primarily paid for by companies since many employees in the Netherlands have a company car as part of their job.
4 It is worth noting that in December 2017 a second VW executive was fined and jailed for the violation. At the sentencing hearing the judge expressed frustration that "senior management has not been held accountable" (Lawrence, 2017). This incident may suggest that regardless of the form and degree of regulation, market pressures will lead to temptations to cheat.

References

Beene, R., Mehrotra, K., & Coppola, G. (2019). Fiat Chrysler Called 'Bad Actor' as U.S. Settles Emissions Suit. _Bloomberg._ Retrieved from https://www.bloomberg.com/news/articles/2019-01-10/fiat-chrysler-agrees-to-pay-fine-recall-vehicles-in-diesel-case

BEIS. (2016). _National atmospheric emissions inventory._ Retrieved from http://naei.beis.gov.uk/overview/pollutants?pollutant_id=6

Canis, B., & Lattanzio, R. K. (2014). _U.S. and EU motor vehicle standards: issues for transatlantic trade negotiations._ Washington, DC. Retrieved from https://www.hsdl.org/?abstract&did=751039

Carey, N., & Shepardson, D. (15 March, 2017). _Big win for automakers as Trump orders fuel economy standards review._ Retrieved from http://www.reuters.com/article/us-usa-trump-autos-idUSKBN16M2C5

Coase, R. (1960). The Problem of Social Cost. _The Journal of Law and Economics_ (October). Retrieved from http://users.uom.gr/~esartz/teaching/envecon/coase.pdf

80 *Vehicle emissions impact*

Davis, J. A. (1963). The California vehicle code and the uniform vehicle code. *Hastings Law Journal, 14*(4), 377–398. Retrieved from https://repository. uchastings.edu/cgi/viewcontent.cgi?article=1744&context=hastings_law_journal

Department for Environment Food and Rural Affairs. (2018). *Public health: sources and effects of PM$_{2.5}$*. London. Retrieved from https://laqm.defra.gov.uk/public-health/pm25.html

Eisenstein, P. A. (March 16, 2017). *Trump Rolls Back Obama-Era Fuel Economy Standards*. Retrieved from http://www.nbcnews.com/business/autos/trump-rolls-back-obama-era-fuel-economy-standards-n734256

EPA. (2018). *Global Greenhouse Gas Emissions Data*. Washington, DC. Retrieved from https://www.epa.gov/ghgemissions/global-greenhouse-gas-emissions-data

European Environment Agency. (2016a). *Explaining road transport emissions: a non-technical guide*. Luxembourg. Retrieved from https://www.eea.europa.eu/publications/explaining-road-transport-emissions

European Environment Agency. (2016b). *The European environment: state and outlook 2015*. Copenhagen: European Environment Agency (EEA). Retrieved from https://www.eea.europa.eu/soer-2015/synthesis/report/0c-executivesummary; https://www.eea.europa.eu/soer

European Environment Agency. (2017). *Air pollution country fact sheet 2017*. Retrieved from https://www.eea.europa.eu/themes/air/country-fact-sheets/united-kingdom

European Union. (2009). *Regulation (EC) No 443 /2009 of the European Parliament and of the Council of 23 April 2009*. Retrieved from https://eur-lex.europa.eu/legal-content/EN/TXT/HTML/?uri=CELEX:32009R0443&from=EN

Eurostat. (2017). *Greenhouse gas emission statistics*. Retrieved from http://ec.europa.eu/eurostat/statistics-explained/index.php/Greenhouse_gas_emission_statistics

Friedlingstein, P., Andrew, R. M., Rogelj, J., Peters, G. P., Canadell, J. G., Knutti, R., . . . Le Quéré, C. (2014). Persistent growth of CO2 emissions and implications for reaching climate targets. *Nature Geoscience, 7*, 709–715. Retrieved from https://www.nature.com/articles/ngeo2248?foxtrotcallback=true. doi:10.1038/ngeo2248

Gately, C. K., Hutyra, L. R., & Wing, I. S. (2015). Cities, traffic, and CO2: a multidecadal assessment of trends, drivers, and scaling relationships. *Proceedings of the National Academy of Sciences, 112*(16), 4999–5004. Retrieved from http://www.pnas.org/content/112/16/4999.abstract. doi:10.1073/pnas.1421723112

Hakim, D., & Mouawad, J. (8 November, 2015). *EPA expands on road emissions testing to all diesel models*. Retrieved from https://www.nytimes.com/2015/11/09/business/energy-environment/epa-expands-on-road-emissions-testing-to-all-diesel-models.html

Holley, P. (2018). Say goodbye to the Ford sedan. *Washington Post*. Retrieved from https://www.washingtonpost.com/news/innovations/wp/2018/04/26/

Vehicle emissions impact 81

ford-has-been-synonymous-with-cars-for-more-than-a-century-thats-about-to-change/?utm_term=.83f912a17d94

Hotten, R. (2015). *Volkswagen: The scandal explained.* 10 December. Retrieved from https://www.bbc.com/news/business-34324772

Kadijk, G., & Ligterink, N. (2012). *Road load determination of passenger cars, The Netherlands Organisation for applied scientific research (TNO).* Retrieved from The Netherlands: https://www.tno.nl/media/1971/road_load_determination_passenger_cars_tno_rl0237.pdf

Krisher, T. (2017). *US says Fiat Chrysler used software to cheat emissions tests.* 23 May. Retrieved from https://phys.org/news/2017-05-fiat-chrysler-software-emissions.html

Lawrence, E. D. (2017). Former Volkswagen manager Oliver Schmidt gets 7 years in diesel emissions cheating scandal. *Detroit Free Press.* Retrieved from https://www.freep.com/story/money/cars/2017/12/06/volkswagen-emission-cheating-scandal-oliver-schmidt-sentencing/924278001/

Majewski, W. A., & Burtscher, H. (2011). *Measurement of Emissions.* Retrieved from https://www.dieselnet.com/tech/measure.php

Mashaw, J., & Harfst, D. (1990). *The Struggle for Auto Safety.* Cambridge, MA: Harvard University Press.

Melosi, M. V. (2004). *The automobile and the environment in American history.* Retrieved from http://www.autolife.umd.umich.edu/Environment/E_Overview/E_Overview4.htm

Mock, P., German, J., Bandivadekar, A., Riemersma, I., Ligterink, N., & Lambrecht, U. (2013). *From Laboratory to Road: A comparison of official and 'real-world' fuel consumption and CO2 values for cars in Europe and the United States.* Retrieved from http://www.theicct.org/sites/default/files/publications/ICCT_LabToRoad_20130527.pdf

Mock, P., Kühlwein, J., Tietge, U., Franco, V., Bandivadekar, A., & German, J. (October, 2014). *The WLTP: How a new test procedure for cars will affect fuel consumption values in the EU.* Retrieved from http://www.theicct.org/sites/default/files/publications/ICCT_WLTP_EffectEU_20141029_0.pdf

Moguen-Toursel, M. (2007). Emergence and transfer of vehicle safety standards: why we still do not have global standards. *Center for Historical Research, Ohio State University, 5,* 4.

NIEHS. (2018). *Climate and Human Health.* Retrieved from https://www.niehs.nih.gov/research/programs/geh/climatechange/health_impacts/index.cfm

Office of Transportation and Air Quality, U. S. E. P. A. (2017). *Welcome to my MPG.* Retrieved from https://www.fueleconomy.gov/mpg/MPG.do

Olsen, P. (2018). GM Becomes Latest Car Company to Drop Some Sedans. *Consumer Reports.* Retrieved from https://www.consumerreports.org/general-motors/gm-to-drop-some-sedans/

Pew Environment Group. (2011). *Cleaner, More Efficient Cars Will Drive Our Nation Toward Energy Independence [Press release].* Retrieved from http://www.pewtrusts.org/~/media/assets/2011/05/11/cafe-fact-sheet-dec2011.pdf

82 *Vehicle emissions impact*

RAC. (2017). *Euro 1 to Euro 6 – find out your vehicle's emissions standard.* Retrieved from https://www.rac.co.uk/drive/advice/know-how/euro-emissions-standards

Snavely, B. (2017). *General Motors may eliminate up six cars lineup report says.* July 22. Retrieved from https://www.usatoday.com/story/money/nation-now/2017/07/22/general-motors-may-eliminate-up-six-cars-lineup-report-says/501847001/

Sorokanich, B. (9 November, 2015). *The EPA Will Finally Conduct Widespread On-Road Emissions Testing.* Retrieved from http://www.roadandtrack.com/new-cars/car-technology/news/a27288/epa-road-testing-vehicle-emissions

Sperling, D. (2018). Trying To Make Sense Of Trump's Rollback Of Vehicle Standards. *Forbes.* Retrieved from https://www.forbes.com/sites/danielsperling/2018/08/02/trying-to-make-sense-of-trumps-rollback-of-vehicle-standards/#52ef6e64e71a

Stephen, R. (2000). *Vehicle of influence: building a European Car Market.* Ann Arbor: University of Michigan Press.

UK Parliament. (2018). *The future relationship between the United Kingdom and the European Union.* London: Presented to Parliament by the Prime Minister by Command of Her Majesty. Retrieved from https://assets.publishing.service.gov.uk/government/uploads/system/uploads/attachment_data/file/725288/The_future_relationship_between_the_United_Kingdom_and_the_European_Union.pdf

UNECE. (2017). Retrieved from http://www.unece.org/trans/main/wp29/faq.html.

United Nations. (1958). *Agreement concerning the adoption of harmonized technical United Nations regulations for wheeled vehicles, equipment and parts which can be fitted and/or be used on wheeled vehicles and the conditions for reciprocal recognition of approvals granted on the basis of these United Nations regulations.* Geneva: United Nations. Retrieved from https://www.unece.org/trans/main/wp29/wp29regs.html

US Department of Energy. (2017). *How vehicles are tested.* Retrieved from http://www.fueleconomy.gov/feg/how_tested.shtml

US Department of Transportation. (2018). *U.S. DOT and EPA Propose Fuel Economy Standards for MY 2021–2026 Vehicles.* Washington, DC. Retrieved from https://www.transportation.gov/briefing-room/dot4818

Vehicle Certification Agency. (2018). *Cars and air pollution.* Retrieved from http://www.dft.gov.uk/vca/fcb/cars-and-air-pollution.asp

von Kaenel, C. (2017). *Auto Sales Hit New Record as Americans Buy More Gas-Guzzling Cars.* Retrieved from https://www.scientificamerican.com/article/auto-sales-hit-new-record-as-americans-buy-more-gas-guzzling-cars/

Williams, M., & Minjares, R. (2016). *A technical summary of Euro 6/VI vehicle emission standards.* Retrieved from https://www.theicct.org/publications/technical-summary-euro-6vi-vehicle-emission-standards

World Bank. (2016). *Air pollution deaths cost global economy 225 billion.* Retrieved from http://www.worldbank.org/en/news/press-release/2016/09/08/air-pollution-deaths-cost-global-economy-225-billion

World Health Organization. (2018). *9 out of 10 people worldwide breathe polluted air, but more countries are taking action.* 2 May. Retrieved from http://www.who.int/news-room/detail/02-05-2018-9-out-of-10-people-worldwide-breathe-polluted-air-but-more-countries-are-taking-action

WSJ. (2018). Market Data Center: Auto Sales. *Wall Street Journal.* Retrieved from http://www.wsj.com/mdc/public/page/2_3022-autosales.html

7 Regulation and the market

The EU's single, 'internal' market is famously based upon four indivisible freedoms: the freedom to move for goods, services, people and capital. This internal market is 'internal' in the sense that there is a common barrier for anything coming into it, and the point of entry does not matter, be it from any location external to that market. But this market is not just 'internal' to the EU because Iceland, Liechtenstein and Norway – states from outside the EU – participate in it through the 1992 European Economic Area agreement, while Switzerland has complicated, separately agreed arrangements providing similar access to the market. Other states have agreements providing for different levels of access to the internal market, or to put this another way, arrangements that enable preferential treatment for their products at the point of entry to the internal market compared to other third countries.

The free movement provisions of the internal market are formulated in two basic approaches. One relates to common standards that apply, and the other deals with the removal of obstacles to trade. For the car industry, both approaches can be seen. Common, centrally set European standards pertain to emissions standards, while the removal of obstacles to trade is clearest in the elimination of tariffs imposed on cars and car parts moving around the market. This is then the central part of the law on the free movement of goods in the EU's market. The Treaties have always considered goods movement as a foundational freedom of the market and have prioritised the removal of obstacles to free trade relating both to price and the quantity of goods traded.

There was much discussion in the debate leading to the Brexit referendum about the level of regulation arising from the EU that is applicable to the UK and UK industry. While it was recognised that the sine qua non of tariff-free access to the market related to agreement on trading terms more broadly, for some who promoted leaving the EU, there was a possibility of achieving tariff-free trade with the EU market without

Regulation and the market 85

having all the regulations that also applied in that market. To others this was a fantasy and better understood as having the cake and eating it (Roberts, 2018). The UK Government seems to have accepted there is an interrelated bond between tariff-free access to the EU market and accepting the regulations applicable in that market – for goods, including cars and car parts, at least – with its proposed withdrawal agreement (UK Government and European Union, 2018). However, the withdrawal agreement appears to be in tatters with multiple rejections by Parliament in addition to ratification risks elsewhere in the EU.

This chapter analyses the market regulations applicable to vehicles and the car industry. Such regulations broadly group either into regulations relating to emissions and those relating to safety. It discusses how regulation and market forces interact and how regulations are often a result of market pressures. One particular dynamic of the car industry is key to European regulations. The car industry, at least in the EU, including the UK, is dependent on complex supply chains, and the industry is in many ways a ballet of logistics and supplier interactions. The chapter sets out the regulations that will continue to apply either, if the UK remains a party to the EU internal market, as a continuing member through the European Economic Area agreement or some tailored equivalent, or through the current Government's withdrawal agreement provisions which will seek to maintain these regulations. Even if the UK leaves this market without a commitment to maintain the regulations, either through the 'no deal' scenario or with an alternative approach that somehow finds a way to have the cake after having eaten it, these regulations will still apply in the EU market and so will affect cars the UK seeks to sell there.

Vehicle technical regulations

Technical regulations, largely relating to safety, underpin one set of vehicle production and manufacture regulations. While many countries have some specific rules that manufacturers are required to follow, there are two primary sets of vehicle commonality rules – the EU requirements and those of the US. These are referred to as homologation requirements.

Most of the technical requirements that will make it difficult for the UK to chart its own course are labelled as regulations to protect citizen safety, although it is sometimes challenging to understand how the degree of these constraints is required for safety. In addition, we will see that the differing requirements between the US and the EU are just that – different, but equally robust. Longitudinal data on road safety demonstrate that the different EU and US systems have the same level of performance and outcomes (Curry, 2016).

86 *Regulation and the market*

US safety standards

In the US, vehicle safety standards are issued by the National Highway Traffic Safety Administration (NHTSA) and are listed in the Code of Federal Regulations Title 49, Subtitle B, Chapter V, Part 571. Collectively they are referred to as the Federal Motor Vehicle Safety Standards (FMVSS) and specify the requirements for manufacturers of motor vehicles and items of motor vehicle equipment. The requirements are specifically identified as necessary to protect the public "against unreasonable risk of crashes occurring as a result of the design, construction, or performance of motor vehicles...and also...against unreasonable risk of death or injury in the event crashes do occur" (NHTSA, 2011, p. ii).

There are 65 vehicle safety standards contained in the FMVSS covering a daunting list of requirements for:

- Controls and displays
- Transmission shift position sequence
- Windshield wiping and washing systems
- Brake systems
- Lamps and reflective devices
- Tyres and rims
- Mirrors
- Hood latches
- Theft protection
- Windows
- Head restraints
- Driver impact protection from the steering system
- Door locks
- Seat belts
- Windshield mounting
- Bumper standards and
- Vehicle identification requirements, just to name a few.

In comparison, the EU has 128 regulations that cover active safety, passive safety and theft plus environmental requirements which in the US are covered in a separate set of requirements (Curry, 2016).

Many of the FMVSS requirements are extensive. For example, Standard 108 covering "Lamps, reflective devices and associated equipment" is nearly 200 pages long and covers everything from the number of lamps to their colour, size, mounting location, mounting height, how they are activated, testing procedures, durability and many, many more. There is no argument that lamps on vehicles are important safety items, but the degree of specificity is extensive and importantly is different from EU requirements. The current US standards differ from the European standards in:

- Glare restrictions
- Focusing of the beam
- Height allowances
- Allowed high beam intensity
- Flexibility to adapt to new technologies such as advanced LED lighting

(Tyler, 2018)

Regulation versus market forces

The vehicle regulatory process is a complicated combination of national priorities, manufacturing interests and idealistic hopes bound up in the ebb and flow of political interests. It is a paradox that the regulatory framework of the EU was developed, in part, to enhance free trade, but only if institutional requirements are met. Extracting from the EU framework will have unintended consequences, and few of those are likely to benefit UK manufacturers. The process of regulatory reform requires careful attention so that desired benefits are not overcome by institutional or firm behaviour (Crampton, 2002). Achieving that balance will be tricky.

Those who believe that markets should dictate outcomes instead of regulators tend to forget that economic theory does not predict that markets will achieve ideal outcomes, because economics does not deal well with normative questions like good and bad. Decisions about what a best outcome in a market should be is a subject for philosophers, ethicists and, perhaps unfortunately in the real world, politicians. Economic theory argues that in a state of perfect knowledge markets will achieve wealth maximising outcomes. But knowledge is not perfect, and as discussed earlier in this text externalities cause costs to be neglected and the lack of defined property rights in such things as the air we breathe mean that markets by themselves are not going to achieve the best outcome, even if there were agreement on what best meant. Regulatory action is also subject to beliefs on the part of those who implement it that will not be accepted by all.

Particularly important for an industry like vehicles that produces complicated products, there is nothing in economic theory that suggests that all markets will express the same preferences which could lead to a costly array of requirements. While they may complain about

88 *Regulation and the market*

excessive bureaucracy, auto manufacturers want uniform requirements to enhance efficiency. This accounts for the angst expressed by vehicle manufacturers each time the Brexit negotiations reflect uncertainty (Campbell & Inagaki, 2016; ITV, 2018). Thus, it is useful to examine specific cases of how markets and the regulatory process have interacted in the motor industry.

Regulation and innovation

Those who argue that regulation stifles innovation in industry ignore history, at least as it applies to the automotive industry. Vehicles are one of the more heavily regulated industries, particularly when it comes to safety and the environment. Yet, history suggests that regulation has lagged innovation. It also shows that innovation is not limited to the auto manufacturers, and they ultimately need to be prodded through regulation into adopting technology that has demonstrated the ability to save lives. Two case studies are representative of how innovations take place.

Centered High Mounted Stop Light

The acronym CHMSL stands for "Centered High Mounted Stop Light". It is the third brake light on cars generally located in the rear window. Its origin is traced back to a taxi company that was experiencing a substantial number of rear end collisions. In 1974 a psychologist who was interested in how a variety of driver interruptions from horns honking to children arguing in the back seat impacted driving behaviour was engaged to perform a test on the company's fleet. The test consisted of installing an additional small brake light in the rear window of 343 taxicabs in San Francisco. Another 160 cabs were not fitted with the lights as a control group. The cabs were then randomly assigned by a dispatcher over a ten-month period to study the impact on collisions. The results were dramatic with a more than 60% reduction in rear-end collisions for the vehicles that were equipped with the light compared with the control group (APA, 2014). It also turned out that the vehicles equipped with the additional light experienced substantially less damage and fewer driver injuries when involved in a collision.

Despite this experimental outcome, no manufacturer expressed interest in implementing this relatively simple technology. It took about a decade for NHTSA to run a similar experiment on a larger scale, and subsequently to mandate the lights for cars sold in the US beginning in 1986, and 1994 for light trucks. It took the EU considerably longer to implement with the regulations not enforcing the CHMSL until 1998 (Rudin-Brown & Jamson, 2013, p. 182).

Data collected in the initial years following implementation did not duplicate the dramatic reductions of the San Francisco experiment, but NHTSA collected information from police data in eight states which did show a 4.3% reduction in rear-end collisions and this extrapolated to "about 200,000 fewer crashes, 60,000 fewer injuries, and more than $600 million in property damage saved every year" (APA, 2014).

Longer-term studies of the CHMSL impact have been less conclusive, with rear-end collisions between 1988 and 2014 increasing by about half a percentage point (Chapman, 2016). But NHTSA argues that the raw data alone can be misleading with a simultaneous increase in drug-impaired driving crashes, and an overall increase in miles driven which leads to more accidents. Of course, now that the vast majority of cars on the road are equipped with CHMSLs, it is difficult to compare outcomes with cars that do not have the lights. Even with the additional data being inconclusive, an insurance institute study concluded that the third brake light is responsible for a 5% reduction in rear-end collisions (Chapman, 2016). In addition, longer-term NHTSA studies calculate that the CHMSL leads to a 4.3% long-term rear-end accident reduction rate based on test findings that the CHMSL significantly reduces driver braking time in response to a signal from the vehicle in front of them (Kahane, 2015, pp. 34, 36). Regardless of the degree of accident prevention, the point relative to innovation is that this simple technology was developed neither by industry, nor the government, and it was only through regulation that it became standard practice.

Electronic Stability Control

A second example of innovation that occurred outside of government regulation, and despite industry reluctance is Electronic Stability Control (ESC). ESC, which is also known by a number of other trade names as sold by different manufacturers, is an extension of a vehicle's braking system that takes control of a skidding situation by sensing a difference between a driver's "intention" and the path the vehicle is taking. The system uses software algorithms to interpret data sent from sensors to the on-board computer and then applies braking to individual or all wheels and will reduce engine power to prevent the vehicle from sliding (Frampton & Thomas, 2007; SRS, 2004). It is also effective in preventing vehicle rollovers. The concept is an extension of antilock braking systems (ABS), an older collision avoidance system in use since

90   *Regulation and the market*

the 1970s. ABS simply stops wheels from spinning during braking by rapidly pulsing brake pressure (Dowling, 2017; Tiwari, 2011).

ESC was in a sense invented by a vehicle manufacturer "by accident". In February 1989 a young engineer who happened to work for Mercedes-Benz skidded off a road in Sweden narrowly missing a row of trees. While awaiting rescue he had time to contemplate what had happened. It occurred to him that antilocking brakes, which had been around for some time but had only recently become widely available, could somehow communicate with the car's computer to instantly measure a car's sideways movement. He was able to convince his bosses to develop the concept, despite the idea being ridiculed by some colleagues.

Following two years of development, a prototype was driven on a test track by a senior company executive, who was known to be a timid driver, and he was able to negotiate an icy obstacle course in a time nearly equal to professional drivers (Dowling, 2017). That led to the decision to put the concept in production, but only as an option on high-end S-class cars. Other manufacturers had begun to test similar technology, but interest in introducing the technology was tepid, in part because of cost considerations, and perhaps also because there was a marketing reluctance to highlight that certain vehicles tended to roll over in the first place. By 2004 suppliers of ESC technology began to complain about the failure of manufacturers to widely introduce the technology (of course they had a vested interest) and they began to go directly to consumers to educate them about the benefits of the system (SRS, 2004). Then in 1997, the technology received an inadvertent boost when a journalist for a Swedish magazine flipped a Mercedes A-Class car while testing the vehicle in what is known as the Moose test where drivers simulate the ability of cars to avoid a collision with these large animals. The A-Class is Mercedes' smallest and least expensive vehicle, so was not fitted with ESC. The wide negative publicity led Mercedes to make the technology standard throughout its line-up. In addition, the company offered the technology free of charge to all manufacturers (Dowling, 2017). The regulators took notice of the public response and the technology became mandatory for cars and light trucks in the US in 2012, and in the EU beginning in 2014 (InterRegs, 2009; NHTSA, 2007).

It is estimated that ESC technology which is now widely disseminated across the globe has saved in excess of a million lives (Dowling, 2017). Studies by numerous researchers and government agencies demonstrated major success well before the technology was required as shown in Table 7.1:

Regulation and the market   91

Table 7.1 Results of selected international studies on the effectiveness of Electronic Stability Control (ESC) before regulation

Country	Study Results
Germany	(2001) ESC could reduce injury accidents by 18% and fatal accidents by 34%
	(2004) More than 25% of injury accidents and 60% of skidding crashes could be prevented by ESC
	45% of accidents where loss of control occurs could be avoided with ESC
Japan	(2003) ESC led to a 35% reduction in single car accidents and a 30% decrease in head-on collisions
Sweden	(2004) 22% reduction in all crashes; 17% reduction on wet or icy roads
USA	(2004) 35% reduction in single vehicle crashes; 30% reduction in single vehicle fatalities
UK	(2007) ESC reduces risk of fatal crashes by 25%, 33% reduction in loss-of-control accidents and 59% decrease in rollover accidents

Sources: EU, 2018; Frampton & Thomas, 2007.

Despite the evidence that the technology saved lives, in the US in 2012 before the regulation, only 20% of cars produced were equipped with ESC (Kahane, 2015, p. 224). It was ultimately regulation that led to widespread adoption, but the regulatory process had nothing to do with the innovation. The fact that it took so long for ESC to become widely implemented and then required is another demonstration that innovation and regulation are only loosely connected. Despite convincing evidence that the technology saves lives, the US National Highway Traffic Safety Administration argues that

> Even a highly effective technology such as ESC needs some years to demonstrate its efficacy, some years of lead-time before it can be built into all new vehicles, and quite a few years before vehicles with ESC replace all the older vehicles on the road that do not have it.
>
> (Kahane, 2015, p. 15)

There is an inherent reluctance for regulators to lead. They will almost always wait for evidence before acting, and then are subject to the political pressures of the time. In data compiled by NHTSA up

92 *Regulation and the market*

to 2012, for 25 safety features on vehicles there was an average lag of seven years between the time the feature was introduced in the market and when it was regulated (Kahane, 2015, p. 220). The argument that the vehicle industry, which among industries is relatively highly regulated, is stymied by these regulations does not hold up.

Interestingly, and a further indication of how regulation is reactive as opposed to proactive, ESC was not made mandatory for large lorries in the US until 2017. These vehicles are perhaps the most likely to experience situations where the braking capability of ESC can prevent serious accidents. However, the rule was finally imposed on manufacturers by the US government (prior to the current administration) over the objections of the Owner-Operator Independent Drivers Association which cited the cost of the systems and claims the government was overestimating the benefits (Jaillet, 2015). Again, regulation did not inhibit the innovations, but the market did not implement the solution as truck owners perhaps undervalued the societal benefit of the technology. Eventually the regulations caught up but played no role in the development of the concept.

Logistics and regulation

Throughout the Brexit debate, both pre and post the referendum, numerous companies and manufacturing associations warned of the importance of the free movement of goods including manufacturing components. That warning has been stated so often it has lost its breaking news value, except to the companies that are impacted. To a vehicle manufacturer it is the difference between operating and closing. The motor industry is the most global industry second only to electronics (IBM, 2008, p. 16). A car has about 20,000 parts. In today's complex logistics chain, they need to arrive not just on a timely basis, but in a near instantaneous basis. Manufacturers do not like to talk about the specifics of their supply chains since they are considered to be competitive advantages, but a study authorised by Chrysler analysing its Jeep plant in Toledo, Ohio, which is typical of large automotive manufacturing facilities, indicated they maintain only one to two hours' inventory of major assemblies. If components fail to arrive, production stops (Vonderembse & Dobrzykowski, 2009, p. 7).

This form of logistics was driven by Toyota. In the early part of the automotive age, vehicles were assembled in factories supplied by thousands of small providers. These firms would deliver components to the assembly operations who would maintain large inventories to ensure they had availability. This writer's hometown of Detroit was dotted with hundreds of small operations that turned out parts and delivered them to the large plants. By the middle part of the 20th century, however, manufacturers took control of fabricating most components through vertical integration. The apex of this process was the Ford Rouge Plant in Dearborn, Michigan which at its high point employed 40,000 workers, and it was said that raw materials would arrive by boat on the Rouge river and vehicles would drive out the other end a few days later.

The Toyota Production System (TPS) evolved over many decades, and began, not with car production, but with mechanical looms. Kiichiro Toyoda, the founder of Toyota Motor Corporation, developed the just-in-time process to eliminate all waste from the production process. Described as a philosophy not just a process, the concept was that all forms of waste including excess inventory eventually clouded management decisions (Toyota, 2018). As Japan was rebuilding from World War II and represented a small element in the automotive industry, these concepts received little notice. However, by the mid-1990s Toyota was expanding rapidly and all manufacturers were forced to embrace these concepts to survive. The evolution of just-in-time production has fundamentally altered the economics of vehicle production. Today, the original equipment manufacturers (OEM) that produce the final product fabricate only those components where they have some compelling competitive advantage to do so. The vast majority of parts are outsourced to a series of what are called tier 1 suppliers who work closely with the OEMs to develop components and are responsible for getting the main components to the assembly plant, not merely in time but sequenced to match the actual order number of the cars that are coming down the line. The economics of this were accentuated by the increasing diversity of products and options that characterise modern vehicles and which require shorter production runs thus making production scheduling more complex. These large suppliers then have secondary and tertiary suppliers who feed their own assembly processes. The entire production and logistics process is complex. The existence of open borders in the EU has supported and accelerated the distribution of components assembly. Brexit risks, at least for the UK, destroying that sequence.

While each manufacturer has its own flavour of the TPS concept, the key point for UK manufacturers post-Brexit (for all manufacturing

94 *Regulation and the market*

processes, not just vehicles) is that any bureaucracy that slows the movement of components, will add to costs and make UK assembly less competitive. The UK automotive manufacturers association reports that in a single day:

- 1,100 trucks arrive in the UK carrying vehicle and engine components
- 5,100 cars are exported
- 5,700 engines are exported

(SMMT, 2018)

The global logistics flow for vehicles is demanding. Clearly, vehicle assembly is not as easy to turn off as it was for Deutsche Bank to shift a part of its euro clearing activity to Frankfurt by flipping a switch (Moore, 2018), but there are key points when decisions will be made about where to locate the next generation of a product, and these will be pragmatic assessments based on cost, regardless of any 'promises' that are made in public relations pronouncements. In February 2018 Toyota "pledged to build the next-generation Auris hatchback at its Derbyshire plant" (Campbell, 2018b). However, in September, when the prospect for a Brexit deal looked suspect the head of Toyota in the UK, Marvin Cooke, began to hedge. He warned that no-deal or a deal with customs and other costs imposed at the border "would add permanent costs to our business. It would reduce our competitiveness. Sadly I think that would reduce the number of cars made in the UK and that would cost jobs" (Togoh, 2018). This voice added to BMW who said it will shut its UK operations if there are customs delays and Vauxhall who has suggested that the Astra plant in Ellesmere Port is at risk (O'Carroll & Topham, 2018). Mercedes added to the rejection list when it announced that before the Brexit vote it had considered moving production to Nissan's Sunderland plant but dropped the idea following the vote (Morrison, 2018).

Markets, regulation and the future

Tariffs are just another form of regulation; a type that contributes to determining economic viability and influencing where production will be based. Free trade in the EU has made it possible for the UK to remain a viable manufacturing location for motor vehicles. If all the components for vehicle assembly were needed to be made in the UK, which would take years to accomplish, the prices of UK manufactured vehicles would rise, and imported cars would become more attractive. Of course, a potential decline in the value of the pound after Brexit would make imported cars more expensive, and in the meantime the prices of imported components for local assembly would increase, further amplifying the impact of border restrictions. Production location decisions in the motor industry are made in discrete chunks. Once implemented they are a challenge to shift short term. But future production decisions will be determined based on expectations of market conditions and the regulatory environment. As a specific example of potential regulatory impact on UK vehicle production, post-Brexit UK-manufactured electric vehicles will not count towards EU CO_2 reduction targets which will be a substantial deterrent to manufacturing in the UK as electric vehicles gain importance in the market (Campbell, 2018a).

As economists are fond of saying – markets work; all government can do is change the incentives and hope the outcomes match the intent. Regulatory impact is like squeezing a balloon; it is impossible to contain all of the unintended consequences that pop out. But the above examples indicate there are situations where regulation benefits society, and situations where markets left free of interference may not embrace efficient solutions. From the perspective of the motor vehicle manufacturing industry in the UK, where international regulations will drive vehicle configurations like safety and pollution controls, it would be better to be inside the decision-making process instead of being independent. Where regulations influence production decisions any outcome other than open borders will disadvantage the UK. This is yet another example of the dichotomy between the desire for UK autonomy and the global reality where manufacturers want certainty, and a single set of requirements is the most efficient path. Brexit is likely to move the UK out of the mainstream.

References

APA. (2014). *Third brake light is no third wheel.* March. Retrieved from https://www.apa.org/action/resources/research-in-action/brake.aspx
Campbell, P. (2018a). No-deal Brexit threatens electric car market. *Financial Times.* Retrieved from https://www.ft.com/content/c45cd3ae-b76a-11e8-bbc3-ccd7de085ffe
Campbell, P. (2018b). Toyota to build next-generation car in Brexit Britain. *Financial Times.* Retrieved from https://www.ft.com/content/b177c726-1c5b-11e8-956a-43db76e69936

96 Regulation and the market

Campbell, P., & Inagaki, K. (2016). UK car factories face uncertain future after Brexit. *Financial Times*. Retrieved from https://www.ft.com/content/27d7b066-447c-11e6-b22f-79eb4891c97d

Chapman, M. (2016). Third brake light: Have rear-end crashes lessened 30 years after mandate? *Chicago Tribune*. Retrieved from http://www.chicagotribune.com/classified/automotive/sc-rear-end-safety-autocover-0901-20160831-story.html

Crampton, P. (2002). *Striking the right balance between competition and regulation: the key is learning from our mistakes*. Paper presented at the APEC-OECD Cooperative Initiative on Regulatory Reform: Third Workshop, Jeju Island, Korea. https://www.oecd.org/regreform/2503205.pdf

Curry, D. (2016). *Automotive regulations & certification processes: a global manufacturer's perspective*. Retrieved from Guayaquil, Ecuador: https://share.ansi.org/Shared%20Documents/Standards%20Activities/International%20Standardization/Standards%20Alliance/Automotive%20Standards%20and%20Regulations%20in%20the%20Americas%20Workshop-%20Ecuador/PowerPoint%20Presentations/D%20Curry%20-%20Industry%20presentation%20-%20April%202022,%202016.pdf

Dowling, J. (2017). Automotive tech breakthrough invented literally by accident. *news.com.au*. Retrieved from https://www.news.com.au/technology/innovation/motoring/automotive-tech-breakthrough-invented-literally-by-accident/news-story/c97bb98f0f2609123d2b73ef84109ee9

EU. (2018). *Electronic stability control*. European Commission. Retrieved from https://ec.europa.eu/transport/road_safety/specialist/knowledge/esave/esafety_measures_known_safety_effects/electronic_stability_control_en

Frampton, R., & Thomas, P. (2007). *Effectiveness of ESC systems*. Retrieved from https://docplayer.net/39174072-Contents-vsrc-loughborough-university-effectiveness-of-esc-systems.html

IBM. (2008). *The enterprise of the future: automotive industry edition*. Retrieved from http://www-935.ibm.com/services/us/gbs/bus/pdf/gbe03122-usen_autoceo.pdf

InterRegs. (2009). *New EC Regulation on General Safety*. Retrieved from https://web.archive.org/web/20141111090411/http://www.interregs.com/spotlight.php?id=84

ITV. (2018). *Jobs warning as Toyota says no-deal Brexit could stall UK car production*. 29 September. Retrieved from http://www.itv.com/news/2018-09-29/job-fears-as-toyota-warns-no-deal-brexit-could-stall-its-uk-car-production/

Jaillet, J. (2015). *ESC mandate published, will take effect August 2017*. 3 June. Retrieved from https://www.ccjdigital.com/esc-mandate-published-will-take-effect-aug-2017/

Kahane, C. J. (2015). *Lives saved by vehicle safety technologies and associated Federal Motor Vehicle Safety Standards, 1960 to 2012 – Passenger cars and LTVs – With reviews of 26 FMVSS and the effectiveness of their associated safety technologies in reducing fatalities, injuries, and crashes*. Washington,

DC: US Department of Transportation Retrieved from https://www-esv. nhtsa.dot.gov/proceedings/24/files/24ESV-000291.PDF

Moore, J. (2018). Brexit means London's financial star is falling. *The Independent*. Retrieved from https://www.independent.co.uk/news/business/ analysis-and-features/brexit-financial-centres-city-of-london-frankfurt-dublin-paris-luxembourg-financial-services-banking-a8471886.html

Morrison, C. (2018). Mercedes-Benz abandoned plans to move production to UK plant after Brexit vote. *The Independent*. Retrieved from https://www. independent.co.uk/news/business/news/mercedes-benz-brexit-production-move-nissan-plant-sunderland-a8568331.html

NHTSA. (2011). *Quick Reference Guide to Federal Motor Vehicle Safety Standards and Regulations*. Washington, DC. Retrieved from https://www.nhtsa. gov/sites/nhtsa.dot.gov/files/fmvss-quickrefguide-hs811439.pdf

NHTSA. (2007). *Federal Motor Vehicle Safety Standards; Electronic Stability Control Systems; Controls and Displays*. Washington, DC: US Department of Transportation. Retrieved from https://www.nhtsa.gov/sites/nhtsa.dot. gov/files/esc_fr_03_2007.pdf

O'Carroll, L., & Topham, G. (2018). Brexit uncertainty puts thousands of jobs at risk, car industry warns. *The Guardian*. Retrieved from https://www. theguardian.com/politics/2018/jun/26/brexit-uncertainty-putting-860000-jobs-at-risk-warns-car-industry

Roberts, D. (2018). Customs row punctures 'have-cake-and-eat-it' Brexit fantasy. *The Guardian*. Retrieved from https://www.theguardian.com/politics/2018/ may/02/customs-squabble-brexit-have-cake-and-eat-it-fantasy

Rudin-Brown, C., & Jamson, S. (2013). *Behavioural adaptation and road safety: theory, evidence and action*. Boca Raton, Florida: CRC Press.

SMMT. (2018). *Key Exports Data*. Retrieved from https://www.smmt.co.uk/ industry-topics/brexit/key-exports-data/

SRS. (2004). *A Brief History of Electronic Stability Control*. 1 July. Retrieved from http://www.safetyresearch.net/blog/articles/brief-history-electronic-stability-controls-and-their-applications

Tiwari, R. (2011). *Traction control systems*. Retrieved from https://cecas. clemson.edu/cvel/auto/AuE835_Projects_2011/Tiwari_project.html

Togoh, I. (2018). No-Deal Brexit Would Stall Toyota UK Production, Putting Jobs At Risk. *Huffington Post*. Retrieved from https://www.huffingtonpost. co.uk/entry/toyota-production-brexit_uk_5baf4b34e4b0343b3dc066c2?-guccounter=1&guce_referrer_us=aHR0cHM6Ly93d3cuZ29vZ2xlLmN-vbS8&guce_referrer_cs=NMIExiH7MwIlPE0JNOXg4g

Toyota. (2018). *The origin of the Toyota Production System*. Retrieved from https://www.toyota-global.com/company/vision_philosophy/toyota_pro-duction_system/origin_of_the_toyota_production_system.html

Tyler, J. S. (2018). *European & American Headlights: How Do They Differ? 9 May*. Retrieved from http://autokredyt.net/european-american-headlights-how-do-they-differ/

98 Regulation and the market

UK Government and European Union. (2018). *Draft Agreement on the withdrawal of the United Kingdom of Great Britain and Northern Ireland from the European Union and the European Atomic Energy Community.* Retrieved from https://ec.europa.eu/commission/publications/draft-agreement-withdrawal-united-kingdom-great-britain-and-northern-ireland-european-union-and-european-atomic-energy-community-agreed-negotiators-level-14-november-2018_en

Vonderembse, M., & Dobrzykowski, D. (2009). *Understanding the Automotive Supply Chain: The Case for Chrysler's Toledo Supplier Park and its Integrated Partners.* Retrieved from Toledo Ohio: http://www.wistrans.org/cfire/documents/AutoSupplyChainCase10_30_09%20FINAL.pdf

8 Disruptors

The Californian Vehicle Code states a "motor vehicle" is a vehicle that is self-propelled but excludes from the scope of the Code "self-propelled wheelchairs, motorised tricycles, and motorised quadricycles, if operated by a person who, by reason of physical disability, is otherwise unable to move about as a pedestrian": USA, Cal. Vehicle Code section 415 (California Legislative Information, 1959). A vehicle is later defined in the Californian code as a means by which a person or property may be propelled, drawn or moved upon a highway or used exclusively upon stationary rails or tracks: USA, Cal. Vehicle Code section 670 (California Legislative Information, 1975). In the UK, the Road Traffic Act 1988 focusses on "a mechanically propelled vehicle, intended or adapted for use on roads" and requires the vehicle carry number plates and be insured if used on public roads (UK Government, 1988). The Australian Personal Property Security Act 2009, as updated by 2014 regulations, includes a minimum speed criterion (Australian Government, 2009). The Australian definition clearly posits the vehicle within the realm of personal property, and even if the Californian and UK approach links the vehicle more closely to movement on public roads, it is implicit that the car is personal property there too.

The previous chapter considered the regulatory framework applicable to cars, and it is then important to define the vehicle to which these regulations apply. But it is also clear that what a motor vehicle is is pretty obvious and not something that requires significant debate or legal definition. It has been a premise of this book that the car is not something that is much different in various parts of the world and this is true because of the market for the car rather than because of rules of definition. However, this premise needs rethinking and that is the focus of this chapter.

The rapid pace of technological development is seeing the introduction of electric vehicles that are ultimately much the same as their motorised precursors but with a different powertrain and are, in some respects, designed with a view to avoiding the complexities

100 *Disruptors*

of emissions standards which have done much to define the industry. Autonomous vehicles are a further step change and they will fundamentally transform the regulatory regime that relates to vehicle safety. Both electric and autonomous vehicles will affect the industry substantially. It is likely some manufacturers will successfully adapt to the new technological environment but even so it is also likely that some cars are going to become out of date rather rapidly. What a motor vehicle, or car, is and what it is understood to be is potentially going to change profoundly as a direct result of technological development.

This chapter considers the development of such innovations and their likely impact. The outcome of the Brexit process will determine the role the UK can play in the future of this industry. The chapter notes the stated commitment by the UK government to be a player in the new industry, specifically by reference to autonomous vehicles, but also recognises investment in the UK in research and development into autonomous vehicles is limited. The technological changes, and the potential for more, are likely to be much more significant in terms of their impact on the car industry than anything agreed relating to the UK's trading relationship with the EU.

The focus in the UK on separation from the EU and the rules of the European market has been widely seen as a distraction from pressing issues facing both the UK itself and the wider EU. Yuval Noah Harari, author of *21 Lessons for the 21st Century* states: "Every minute the British and EU institutions are spending on negotiations is a minute they don't spend on climate change. And they spend a lot of minutes on Brexit" (The Irish News, 2018). If the big threat is climate change, issues of national sovereignty will become largely meaningless. Specifically relating to the motor vehicle industry, national industries face a profound challenge with technological change. The ability of the UK to chart an independent path for the automotive sector and secure trade deals to enhance sector employment appears to be, from the government's White Paper, based on the assumption that the world will be static. In the previous chapter, it was noted that the ability of the UK to change the rules of the game when it comes to vehicle regulations will be minimal. The UK may achieve agreements that test procedures and results will be accepted post-Brexit, but that will not apply to future changes in the rules. Even this level of agreement, however, is unlikely to persist because the environment itself is almost certainly going to change. The vehicle industry is entering a period of greater structural change than it has seen in a century. A recent KPMG report stated: "The auto industry is lost in translation between evolutionary, revolutionary and disruptive key trends that all need to be managed at the same time" (KPMG, 2017). Some of those changes may actually enhance prospects for the UK vehicle industry depending on how they play out; others will not. While the industry would argue that it is always undergoing change and they have effectively managed and even led the change, the upcoming disruptions to the status quo will be challenging.

Electric vehicles and autonomous vehicles are considered in separate sections below. While these are in some ways distinct technological issues, they are closely related by the form in which they are likely to evolve and coexist. We will examine these two sets of changes individually before considering their interface.

Electric vehicles

It is important to remember that the car itself was a disruptor whose impact fundamentally changed society. When the first "horseless carriages" were introduced in the later part of the 19th century they were considered playthings for the wealthy. The contraptions were exactly as they were named – things that did what carriages did minus the hooves (Davies, 2018b). The word car was already in the English language, but generally referred to any horse-drawn vehicle with wheels (Ray, 2016). It took decades for the word to transition to motorised vehicles exclusively, and for the horseless moniker to disappear.

The history of the electric car significantly precedes that of internal combustion engine vehicles. In the 1830s the Scottish inventor Robert Anderson developed the first electric vehicle. However, since it ran on non-rechargeable primary cells, it was hardly practical. Two French inventors moved the technology forward in the 1880s. Gaston Planté invented rechargeable lead-acid storage; subsequently Camille Faure improved the battery's ability to supply current and effectively created the basic lead-acid battery used in standard vehicles today (PBS, 2009). With the lack of an viable alternative, the electric car achieved dominance in what was, admittedly, a tiny market. Electric vehicles also benefitted from the fact that, especially in urban areas, horses were a nuisance and expensive to maintain (Kilson, 2016).

The first petrol-fuelled four-stroke engine was invented in 1876, and a decade later the first commercial production of internal combustion engine vehicles began by Carl Benz (Melosi, 2010). During this period, the electric engine largely competed with vehicles powered by steam. Electric vehicles had a clear advantage over steam cars in ease of use and safety. In addition, they were well suited to urban transportation before the development of extensive road systems (Kilson, 2016).

102 *Disruptors*

Thomas Edison considered the promise of electric cars to be so great that in 1899 he began a decade long attempt to develop a long-lasting battery to power vehicles. He promised that the problem of poor battery storage capacity was about to be solved. While he managed to make a few improvements to alkaline batteries, by 1910 he had abandoned his effort to solve the fundamental problem that would plague electric vehicles to this day – the cord is too short.

This dilemma is demonstrated by the growth of battery storage limits. At the end of the 19th century battery capacities were about 10 watt-hours per kilogram (Wh/kg). By 1911 it had expanded to about 25 Wh/kg. From this point improvement slowed dramatically, and over the next 80 years the capacity only doubled (Cowan & Hulté, 1996). It was the invention of the lithium ion battery in the 1970s and widely available at the end of the 20th century that brought renewed promise for electric vehicles.

Improvements in the internal combustion engine during the 1890s are also generally credited with killing electric vehicles. Indeed, the basic concepts of the internal combustion engine were effectively refined to such an extent during that time that there have been many improvements, but no fundamental change in the principles of automobile engines since then (Melosi, 2010). Thus, the introduction of the Ford Model T in 1908 is regarded to be the end of the early electric vehicle age in part because a Model T cost about a third of the average price of an electric vehicle (Erich & Witteveen, 2017). However, the original Model T still suffered from the problem of being able to start easily. The hand crank process needed to start the engine required strong arms, and frequently resulted in injuries. Therefore, it is perhaps more appropriate to credit Charles Kettering's invention of the first practical electric starter in 1912 as the true end of electric vehicles' popularity (PBS, 2009).

It also turned out that steam and electric vehicles were hurt by poor marketing and manufacturing choices that benefitted the combustion engine. Petrol vehicle manufacturers moved far more quickly to introduce mass production than did steam or electric vehicle companies. By the start of the 20th century, the Stanley brothers were the leading producer of steam cars, and they were content with producing only about 700 high-end cars a year. They rejected mass production and did not like to advertise. From this limited volume they were able to make a good living but consigned their product to the footnotes of history. Likewise, electric vehicle manufacturers were more interested in selling up-end vehicles. In 1914, the average price of an electric vehicle was more than four times that of a Ford (Cowan & Hulté, 1996).

Over the decades of the 20th century and into the 21st century, there have been many attempts to revive electric vehicles, principally in the form of hybrid vehicles that combine electric power with either a petrol or diesel engine. In addition, the development and refinement of lithium ion batteries with greater power and longer life between charges has again raised hopes that electric cars will become the future of the motor industry. Today, every major automotive manufacturer has an electric vehicle in its portfolio. If a major transition occurs, what impact will this disruption in the composition of the market have on a post-Brexit UK motor industry?

Not only manufacturers, but governments are jumping on the electric bandwagon. As one of the components of the UK government's Industrial Strategy, it sets out a four element Grand Challenge of which The Future of Mobility is a part. The stated mission of the mobility challenge is to: "Put the UK at the forefront of the design and manufacturing of zero emission vehicles, with all new cars and vans effectively zero emission by 2040" (UK Department of Business Industry & Industrial Strategy, 2018). To support the mission the government has committed to a £1 billion investment to back the development of low carbon powertrains and £246 million to create effective batteries for electric vehicles. In addition, the government will provide grants to assist consumers in buying electric cars and will develop the battery charging infrastructure. While most of the investment is conditioned on matching investment from industry, manufacturers have bought into the plan by helping to develop and supporting the *Automotive Sector Deal*, a component of the Industrial Strategy (HM Government, 2018).

First, a caution against too much electric optimism. Despite the hype by proponents, electric vehicles are not on the verge of wiping out the internal combustion engine. It took decades for the infrastructure of roads and fuelling stations to support the transportation system of today, and while the road structure will be in place for electric vehicles, refuelling will require substantial investment. And, refuelling will be critical, for while proponents tout the range of their vehicles, the facts are more restrained. The range for the principal electric cars on the market before requiring a recharge is shown in Table 8.1.

Table 8.1 Selected 2018 model year electric vehicle ranges between charges (miles)

BMW i3	114	Kia Soul	111
Chevrolet Bolt EV	238	Nissan Leaf	151
Fiat 500e	84	Smart Fortwo	58
Ford Focus	115	Tesla S100D	335
Hyundai Ionic	124	VW e-Golf	83

Source: US EPA Fuel Economy Guide Model Year 2018.

104 *Disruptors*

The above data comes with all kinds of qualifications that the range rating in an electric vehicle is sensitive to driving styles, weather conditions and use of equipment. It is also true that various testing sites have different values for the range, and manufacturers' sites often have higher values than shown above. However, as an independent source the EPA ranges are a reasonable approximation. The measured ranges have been rising over time as technology improves, but petrol versions of the above vehicles would typically have fuel ranges between refuelling of 300–400 miles. Currently only Tesla approaches this level. A survey of 52,000 Dutch drivers suggested that the range of electric cars would have to attain a similar level to petrol engines before a majority would be willing to consider an electric vehicle (Erich & Witteveen, 2017, p. 7). This is not going to happen overnight, but despite more than a century of electric vehicle disappointments the general view is that sometime between 2025 and 2040 electric cars will replace the internal combustion engine (Le Petit, 2017).

This view is not, however, universal. A 2017 survey of nearly 1,000 senior global automotive executives indicted that more than 60% of them believe that the traditional battery electric vehicle concept will fail because the infrastructure will not develop to support these cars. Three quarters of the respondents, however, believe that hydrogen fuel cells will be the development that will create the electric vehicle revolution. These executives believe that fuel cell vehicles that could be refuelled quickly at traditional petrol stations will make even a 25-minute recharging time for lithium ion batteries seem unreasonable (KPMG, 2017, p. 14). However, the impact on the UK motor industry resulting from the success of electric vehicles of either type will be similar, so this text will concentrate on the currently popular battery format.

Another challenge for electric vehicles that will likely benefit the UK motor industry in the medium term is that electric vehicles suffer from what has been described as a 'lock-in' situation (David, 1985). The petrol engine, having established a position of dominance, will be difficult to replace even if electric vehicles achieve performance parity. Despite the UK government's support for electric vehicle infrastructure mentioned above, the entire societal infrastructure is in place to support internal combustion vehicles. As a classic example related to a different product, there have been numerous studies that have shown conclusively that the standard QWERTY keyboard that is being used to produce this text is inefficient. Yet, despite overwhelming evidence to this fact, all attempts to replace QWERTY have failed miserably. This is partly because of a lack of incentives for any one business to

Disruptors 105

invest in training to implement this productivity enhancement combined with the difficulty of reversing an intrenched investment (David, 1985, pp. 334–335). Unless there is a regulation enforcing change, or a technological leap so advanced that consumers cannot afford to remain with their current choices, inertia will prevail.

An additional challenge beyond the actual range of electric vehicles is the time required to recharge the battery. Here the data can be confusing and various sources are contradictory. But using US Environmental Protection Agency data there are three types of charging:

- Level 1: Plugged into a household 120-volt outlet yields about 2–5 miles of range per hour of charging.
- Level 2: Plugged into a 240-volt charging device yields 10–30 miles of range per hour of charging.
- DC Fast Charging: Allows about 50 miles of range for 20 minutes of charging, but not all vehicles can accept this type of charge.

(EPA, 2018)

The specialised DC Fast Charge uses a high-level DC current, generally up to 120 kW, directly to the vehicle's battery without passing through an onboard AC/DC converter. However, most drivers would not be pleased to hang around a charging station for 20 minutes at a time to get 50 miles of driving or plugging their vehicle in for up to eight hours to get a full charge. For most, the cord remains too short, and despite continual promises of better range to come there do not appear to be any immediate technological improvements to double or triple current electric vehicle performance. It also should be noted that while emissions of electric vehicles are zero, the emissions of producing the electricity are not, and battery disposal has its own environmental issues, but those are not central to Brexit.

Despite the abovementioned challenges to the rapid growth of EVs, there is no question that they are growing. No longer are they one-off products to test the market. Electric vehicles are being produced by virtually all major manufacturers, and even though the volumes are still relatively small, the list of new EV product launches for 2019 is indicative that these products are moving towards the mainstream:

- Audi E-tron Quattro
- Hyundai Kona
- Hyundai Nexo (fuel-cell)
- Jaguar I-Pace
- Kia Niro

106 *Disruptors*

- Lucid Air
- Mercedes-Benz EQC
- Porsche Taycan
- Range Rover Sport (hybrid)

(Browne, 2019)

What the consequences of a post-Brexit electric vehicle transition will be is unclear even considering that the day of the electric vehicle takeover is some time down the road. However, even if there were no Brexit, a transition to electric vehicles it will result in a significant decrease in manufacturing jobs. This is because electric vehicles are simpler products to manufacture and have far fewer components. In a sense, electric vehicles are iPads with wheels. Engines, exhausts and many transmission components will be replaced by batteries, smaller electric engines and numerous electronics. A typical internal combustion powertrain today has 1,400 parts; an equivalent electric vehicle will have 200 (Erich & Witteveen, 2017). There will not be the need for as many manufacturing jobs. Credit Suisse estimates that vehicle manufacturing will need 18% fewer workers as electric production takes hold (Bryant, 2019). In the case of Germany, a recent study suggested that a rapid shift to electric vehicle production would put 600,000 jobs at risk (Bormann & Fink, 2018, p. 18).

Data from ING Bank indicates that a third of the value chain for vehicle production is at risk with electric vehicles. This results from the simpler nature of electric vehicle production in addition to having fewer components overall. For an internal combustion vehicle, the estimated average annual number of engine components produced by an employee is 350, with a similar number for transmissions. The average annual production of components for electric vehicles is 1,600 (Erich & Witteveen, 2017, p. 13). There will be additional requirements for raw materials, mainly for battery production, but this does not begin to offset the reduced requirements for manufacturing labour. There is also a risk that many of the remaining manufacturing jobs will be lower skilled and thus lower paying (Bormann & Fink, 2018, p. 18).

Of course, reduced jobs in the automotive industry does not mean that the economic effects of an electric car conversion will be negative for the UK, Brexit or not. Electric vehicles could lead to an additional 19,000 jobs in the UK for research and development, infrastructure creation and additional general consumer spending resulting from lower transportation costs for vehicle users (Le Petit, 2017). However, those impacts are outside the scope of this work.

The eventuality of autonomous vehicles

The second major disruptor to the vehicle industry that will occur in the near future is the autonomous vehicle (AV). For more than 100 years the car has played a major role not only in how people operate in their daily lives, but also in the evolution of our culture. The achievement of a driving license is a rite of passage. Even though recent studies have shown a noticeable decline in the percentage of younger people who are choosing to become licensed drivers, cars remain a powerful social symbol.[1] This is likely another reason why sustaining the motor vehicle industry in the UK receives extensive attention.

As with the electric vehicle it is useful to review the history of autonomous vehicles to understand how they are likely to affect the UK vehicle industry, and its ability to chart its own course post-Brexit. The history of autonomous vehicles is far shorter than that for electric vehicles. Despite science fiction and popular culture visions of vehicles that required no human intervention the concept was not taken seriously until the 1980s. Autonomous vehicles were always considered a futuristic idea, and forecasts of the introduction of driverless vehicles always appeared to be a concept that was near but in the future. The vision was driven by the skyrocketing number of vehicle-related deaths beginning in the 1920s, and the idea of taking away control from humans was always seen as the way to reduce the carnage. However, as recently as a decade ago few people thought that the potential for AVs was any closer than it had been in the past (Davies, 2018b).

The basis of the current acceleration in the development of driverless cars was driven by military interest. The first "driverless" car was tested at a military airfield in Ohio in the US in 1921 (Kröger, 2016, p. 43). Technically this was a remote-controlled vehicle in that a person with a radio device walked a few metres behind the car. In 1925 an actual car was driven remotely in New York City, but again as a remote-controlled vehicle. The 1960 World's Fair presented an elaborate ride called *Futurama* that depicted automated highways. How this future was to be realised was always indistinct. The main idea starting from the 1930s was that guide wires would be buried in the pavement, and that vehicles would communicate with these wires and be led safely along the highway. The guide wire concept remained the focus of development until the 1970s. A one-mile demonstration road was set up by General Motors in 1958 that provided good public relations, but no feasibility. Meanwhile popular culture frequently featured autonomous vehicles, often in an anthropomorphic format. From Walt Disney's loveable Herbie the racing Beetle to *Christine*, a 1983 horror

108 *Disruptors*

film adaptation of a Steven King novel where the car's owner is possessed by the vehicle and goes hunting, to the 1982–1986 TV series *Knight Rider* where the protagonist's vehicle named KITT (Knight Industries Two Thousand) not only helps solve crimes, but also protects its owner by refusing to engage in overly dangerous actions, autonomous vehicles were presented as humanoid beings with minds of their own, but not as realistic possibilities (Kröger, 2016, pp. 57–60).

Meanwhile, the real world began to abandon true autonomy in favour of gradual approaches that assisted drivers with devices and would sometimes take control. Features in this group included cruise control (1958), anti-lock braking (ABS, 1978), electronic skid control systems (ESP, 1995) and the TomTom GPS system (2004). These and other items have gradually worked their way into mainstream vehicles, but users rarely think of them as options that automate their vehicles.

While there were numerous developments leading to true autonomous vehicles beginning in the 1970s, including a TV-controlled cart developed by Stanford University in 1979 that managed to independently move through rooms with furniture, but at a speed of 1 metre every 10–15 minutes (Kröger, 2016, p. 59), the major push that led to the current wave of autonomous vehicle development was instituted by the US Department of Defense in a programme called the Defense Advanced Research Programs Agency (DARPA) challenge. The military recognised the potential of having unmanned vehicles being able to enter combat zones in rugged territory. Having failed on their own to develop successful vehicles, the government offered a $1 million prize for an unmanned vehicle to traverse a 240 km course in the California desert. The first challenge in 2004 was something of a fiasco with the longest surviving vehicle making it less than 12 km (Davies, 2017).

The bright side of the initial challenge was that it generated a lot of interest and collaboration in research labs around the world to surmount the many challenges that confront autonomous vehicles, and many of those involved in that initial challenge are leading the industry today. The question for the UK is how will it fit in as the industry, still in its infancy, evolves? Will Brexit provide an opportunity to offset the potential challenges to manufacturing that will be posed by electric vehicles?

The fact is that autonomous vehicles, despite a long history of fantasy and visionary prospects, are only beginning to be perceived as something that could become reality soon. A well-known theory of product development, called the Innovation S-Curve, tracks the typical progress of new products. Figure 8.1 represents this pattern.

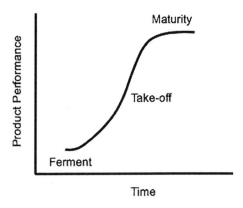

Figure 8.1 Innovation S-Curve.
Source: van Wyk, 1987.

The start of the S-curve is the ferment stage. Here the product is completely new, and no market has been established. There will be a lot of jockeying for position by innovators/competitors, but the evolution of the product is yet unclear. Take-off occurs when the main technological obstacles have been overcome, a dominant structure of the product confirmed, and consumers move quickly to acquire the product. Time frames may vary, and of course innovation continues to occur, but the product gains approval, or not, and production will grow rapidly. Eventually the market attains maturity, production slows, and customers wait for the next major thing that will start a new S-curve (van Wyk, 1987, p. 348). Following decades of thought and visualisation, autonomous vehicles remain in the ferment stage, but it must be said that the take-off portion of the curve appears imminent. Waymo, a company spun off from Google's self-driving car project has improved the pedestrian-detection capability of its vehicles recently by a factor of a hundred (Vanderbilt, 2018, p. 82). Waymo's self-driving cars have now navigated 10 million miles in 25 cities.

The UK has announced that they intend to be a leader in autonomous vehicles. The government recognises the importance of autonomous vehicles and wants them in commercial use by 2021. On-road testing is planned or being performed in Greenwich, Beckton, Oxford, Coventry, Milton Keynes, Bristol and elsewhere (Burgess, 2018). However, this is a minor effort compared to the more than £60 billion that manufacturers and research labs are estimated to have spent

110 *Disruptors*

through the end of 2017 (Loveday, 2018). Nvidia, the leading producer of Graphic Processing Units (GPU) that have become central to the ability for autonomous vehicles to distinguish between humans and inanimate objects, has more than 200 companies working with its automotive unit to enhance this technology. Research is being conducted by virtually every global vehicle manufacturer and there is major investment by non-automotive companies such as Amazon, Apple and Baidu, the Chinese internet giant (CBInsights, 2018). The UK is not leading in this area.

And, despite the statements of interest, the UK government has announced a hands-off policy in terms of establishing rules and regulations impacting the development and use of autonomous vehicles. In a March 2018 letter to the House of Lords Baroness Sugg said

> Whilst we do know that there will be different types of automated vehicles, with varying levels of sophistication, it is not possible at this stage to state what those changes will be. With this in mind it would not be appropriate to set definitive regulations in legislation at this time.
>
> (Corfield, 2018; Sugg, 2018)

It certainly can be argued that a strict legislative approach can stifle investment and creativity, but the fact is that the world is developing legislative frameworks for AVs and, as has been argued elsewhere in this text, the UK is going to be bound by the rules developed elsewhere.

To examine the areas where legislation and regulation will shape the development of autonomous vehicles it is helpful to understand the different levels of AV operation. The Society of Automotive Engineers (SAE) has defined five progressive levels of autonomous driving which have been accepted as the standard by the US National Highway Traffic and Safety Administration (NHTSA) (Litman, 2018; Loveday, 2018):

1   Driver Assistance: specific execution to assist steering or acceleration/deceleration such as adaptive cruise control or lane centring. The driver performs all remaining functions.
2   Partial Driving Automation: execution to assist adaptive cruise control and lane centring.
3   Conditional Automation: automated driving at low speeds in dense traffic. The driver must take over after a warning issued by the system.

Disruptors 111

4 High Automation: Automated driving in a defined city centre. If the system runs into trouble it brings the vehicle to a safe stop.
5 Full Automation: Full time performance by an automated system of all aspects of on-road driving. If the system stops working, it will bring the vehicle to a safe stop.

Levels 1 and 2 require the full attention of the driver to the road. In levels 3 through 5, the vehicle monitors the environment allowing the driver to take his/her eyes off the road, perhaps even sleeping in levels 4 and 5. It is level 4 that most manufacturers are targeting with level five seen as a more distant future (Loveday, 2018). Each of these levels of automation raise questions for the legal and regulatory environment as vehicle systems will be making potentially life and death decisions. As a vehicle moves through traffic, even with the finest technology, there will inevitably be 'dilemma situations' where an accident will occur. Traditional legal systems place fault on a driver, a technical failure or environmental situations (Beiker, 2012). Liability cannot be placed on a machine. The way the vehicle makes these decisions will be based on programming to minimise the loss of human life, but the ethical approach to determine how those decisions will be made is far from clear (Gerdes & Thornton, 2016, p. 101). The legal system has yet to figure out how to assess liability. Decisions about how to assess liability will alter, and potentially slow, the development of autonomous driving.

As an example, in March 2018 a self-driving UBER test vehicle struck and killed a woman in the US state of Arizona. This caused UBER to temporarily halt AV testing. Following investigation, the Arizona police reported that the human behind the wheel of the vehicle who was supposed to be monitoring the driving was in fact streaming video on her phone. The human monitor may face charges that could include manslaughter, which is the way the legal system operates today, but it may well be that the assigned task was destined to lead to an unfortunate result. Research conducted during World War II by the RAF to ascertain how long young men could monitor screens in search of enemy craft determined attention wandered in less than 30 minutes (Davies, 2018a). Humans may not be well suited to the tedious task of observing autonomous vehicle operation. However this case is resolved, and those of future mishaps, the outcomes determined by lawyers will guide the development path of autonomous vehicles. These decisions will take place all over the world, but will be solidified by the large players, principally the EU, the US and China. UK independence will not be an advantage in this development.

112 *Disruptors*

Insurance and AVs

Another automotive related industry product that will be affected by autonomous vehicles is insurance. This may appear initially as tangential to any Brexit decision, but we argue that this UK industry will be impacted by the way AV manufacturing processes evolve. The UK insurance industry is the largest in Europe, and automotive insurance is a major part of that, paying out more than £12 billion in claims each year (ABI, 2017). This industry has a stake in how autonomous vehicle rules will be defined, and the resulting impact on liability, offerings and profits. Liability rules today are derived from a century's worth of legal cases, legislation and industry practice. Autonomous vehicles will throw much of that into question.

As an autonomous vehicle moves along the road, it will make millions of decisions, none of which are in the control of, and thus the responsibility of, the vehicles' occupants (Beiker, 2012). How can liability be assigned? If you cannot blame the occupants, and you cannot blame the car, then the residual option is to blame the owner. In fact, the decisions the vehicle makes in dilemma situations will have been made, at least partially, by programmers. Ethicists have been weighing in on these types of decisions long before autonomous vehicles were conceived. If an accident is inevitable, perhaps because a child darts out from behind a parked vehicle that no scanner would detect until it is too late to avoid a collision, and the AV faces a choice of killing the child or veering into an oncoming lorry with potential loss of all lives in both vehicles, what is the 'right choice'? Different configurations of this type of dilemma elicit different responses from humans depending on how the question is posed (Thomson, 1985). It is impractical to assign liability to the thousands of programmers who will at one point or another develop code. And, in fact, through artificial intelligence, machines will assimilate experience and derive outcomes that the programmers would never have considered. Recent research with artificial intelligence playing an abstract strategy game called Go demonstrate that the computer will make moves never contemplated by human game masters, and the machine is learning from itself as it plays more games (Vincent, 2017).

In a sense, an autonomous vehicle will be playing a continuous video game, amassing points by choosing options based on computer choices, some of which are pre-programmed, and others 'learned' by the vehicle as it operates. The fact is that there are no clear-cut answers to some of the choices these vehicles will be forced to make. Ethical questions such as whether an AV should stay on course and kill several pedestrians or whether to swerve and kill its own passenger could, in theory, even be established by the occupants of a vehicle through an ethical knob on the dashboard that would implement priorities at the start of each trip (Contissa, Lagioia, & Sartor, 2017). The insurance industry will face substantial challenges as autonomous vehicles develop.

Some experts believe that at least initially the problem should be circumvented by having autonomous vehicles owned and insured by the manufacturer (Loveday, 2018). This could help establish trust in the vehicles while experience is being accumulated, rules become established and case law is developed. This would presumably lead to a major expansion of ride sharing. If autonomous vehicles do become virtually accident-free, then there would likely be a major reduction in vehicle insurance premiums that would then focus on comprehensive coverage, and this would in turn have an impact on employment in the insurance industry. Evidence collected from the as yet limited set of autonomous options offered on some vehicles confirms that accident rates will be lowered as autonomy takes over (Clements & Kockelman, 2017, p. 9). So, Brexit or not, autonomous vehicles are going to impact this industry, and the way the rules develop will inform the development of the vehicles. As a domestic industry Brexit need not have a major impact on how the liability rules evolve in the country and impact insurance companies, but the vehicle manufacturing industry will be impacted by technical requirements that evolve from regulation and case law in the larger markets, so even here the UK will lose influence if it is not in the decision-making process.

Adding electric to the AV mix

It is likely that as autonomous vehicles progress through the five stages of automation electric vehicles will become a predominant element. This is because autonomous vehicles will develop their capabilities initially in urban traffic where electric cars have advantages because distances are shorter and speeds are slower. The more electric vehicles produced, the lower the level of manufacturing employment required. The more autonomous technology is implemented, the greater the potential for ride-sharing implementation that will conveniently and economically allow people to move around urban centres without having to bother with parking. Thus, these two disruptors will become complementary, enhancing each other's growth.

Societal forces may also induce these disruptors to combine. If autonomous vehicles actually increase the amount of travel by making it more convenient, then unless autonomy is combined with electric vehicles the amount of pollution and carbon emitted will increase (Union

114 *Disruptors*

of Concerned Scientists, 2017). Consequently, while electric vehicles and autonomous vehicles are separate technical innovations, they are linked. And, just as the invention and development of the 'horseless carriage' transformed the landscape of society, the next generation of transportation development could have major impacts on life. Brexit or not, neither electric vehicles nor autonomous vehicles are positive for maintaining the current size of motor industry manufacturing in the UK. Each of these technologies match all of the criteria that the United Nations Economic Commission for Europe (UNECE) established for considering items that were to be subject to harmonisation: public safety and health, ecology, energy efficiency and areas where the lack of harmonised standards might create technical obstacles to international trade (UNECE, 2002). The UNECE rules for current vehicle standards are accepted in most countries of the world to define how vehicles must operate. It is likely that this organisation, historically led by the EU, will define the rules for upcoming generations. It will be the EU, not independent countries, that will develop those rules.

Note

1 In the UK the percentage of men aged 21–29 who are licensed drivers declined from 80% in 1996 to 67% in 2009. Overall, however, the percentage of males between the ages of 40 and 60 who have access to a car remains near 90% (Goodwin, 2012, pp. 16–17).

References

ABI. (2017). *UK Insurance & Long-term Savings Key Facts.* Retrieved from https://www.abi.org.uk/data-and-resources/industry-data/uk-insurance-and-long-term-savings-key-facts/

Australian Government. (2009). *Personal Property Securities Act 2009.* Canberra. Retrieved from https://www.ppsr.gov.au/ppsr-overview

Beiker, S. A. (2012). Legal aspects of autonomous driving. *Santa Clara Law Review, 52*(1145), 1152–1156.

Bormann, R., & Fink, P. (2018). *The future of the German automotive industry transformation by disaster or by design?* (ISBN: 978-3-96250-100-6). Retrieved from Bonn, Germany: http://library.fes.de/pdf-files/wiso/14450.pdf

Browne, W. (2019). *US Light Vehicle Flash Report.* Retrieved from Detroit: wpbrownellc@yahoo.com

Bryant, C. (2019). Where Ford and Jaguar Lead, the Rest Will Surely Follow: The carmakers are struggling with the epochal change to electric motors. Expect thousands more job losses in the next decade. *bloomberg.com.* Retrieved from https://www.bloomberg.com/opinion/articles/2019-01-10/ford-and-jaguar-land-rover-job-cuts-are-just-the-start

Burgess, M. (2018). *Driverless car testing in the UK*. 30 August. Retrieved from https://www.wired.co.uk/article/driverless-cars-uk-self-driving-cars

California Legislative Information. (1959). *California Vehicle Code: Section 415*. California: State of California. Retrieved from https://leginfo.legislature.ca.gov/faces/codes_displaySection.xhtml?lawCode=VEH&sectionNum=415

California Legislative Information. (1975). *Vehicle Code 670*. Sacramento California: State of California. Retrieved from https://leginfo.legislature.ca.gov/faces/codes_displaySection.xhtml?lawCode=VEH&sectionNum=670

CBInsights. (2018). 46 corporations working on autonomous vehicles. 4 September. Retrieved from https://www.cbinsights.com/research/autonomous-driverless-vehicles-corporations-list/

Clements, L. M., & Kockelman, K. M. (2017). Economic effects of automated vehicles. *Transportation Research Record, No. 2602, 2017*. Retrieved from https://www.caee.utexas.edu/prof/kockelman/public_html/TRB17EconomicEffectsofAVs.pdf.

Contissa, G., Lagioia, F., & Sartor, G. (2017). The Ethical Knob: ethically-customisable automated vehicles and the law. *Artificial Intelligence and Law, 25*(3), 365–378. doi:10.1007/s10506-017-9211-z

Corfield, G. (2018). *UK.gov: We're not regulating driverless vehicles until others do*. 4 April. Retrieved from https://www.theregister.co.uk/2018/04/04/ukgov_driverless_car_regulation/

Cowan, R., & Hulté, S. (1996). *Escaping Lock-in: the Case of the Electric Vehicle*. Retrieved from http://citeseerx.ist.psu.edu/viewdoc/download?doi=10.1.1.522.9381&rep=rep1&type=pdf

David, P. A. (1985). Clio and the Economics of QWERTY. *The American Economic Review, Vol. 75, No. 2, Papers and Proceedings of the Ninety-Seventh Annual Meeting of the American Economic Association. (May, 1985), pp. 332–337, 75*(2), 332–337. Retrieved from https://econ.ucsb.edu/~tedb/Courses/Ec100C/DavidQwerty.pdf

Davies, A. (2017). *An oral history of the DARPA grand challenge, the grueling robot race that launched the self-driving car*. 3 August. Retrieved from https://www.wired.com/story/darpa-grand-challenge-2004-oral-history/

Davies, A. (2018a). *The unavoidable folly of making humans train self-driving cars*. 22 June. Retrieved from wired.com

Davies, A. (2018b). *The Wired guide to self-driving cars*. 17 May. Retrieved from https://www.wired.com/story/guide-self-driving-cars/

EPA. (2018). *Fuel economy guide 2018 model year*. Washington, DC. Retrieved from https://www.fueleconomy.gov/feg/pdfs/guides/FEG2018.pdf

Erich, M., & Witteveen, J. (2017). *Breakthrough of electric vehicle threatens European car industry July*. Retrieved from https://www.ingwb.com/media/1994284/ing-breakthrough-of-electric-vehicle-threatens-european-car-industry.pdf

Gerdes, J. C., & Thornton, S. M. (2016). Implementable ethics for autonomous vehicles. In M. Maurer, J. C. Gerdes, B. Lenz, & H. Winner (Eds.), *Autonomous driving: technical, legal and social aspects* (pp. 87–103). Berlin: Springer.

116 Disruptors

Goodwin, P. (2012). Peak travel, peak car and the future of mobility: evidence, unresolved issues, and policy implications, and a research agenda. In International Transport Forum Discussion Papers, OECD Publishing.

HM Government. (2018). *Industrial strategy: automotive sector deal.* London. Retrieved from https://assets.publishing.service.gov.uk/government/uploads/system/uploads/attachment_data/file/673045/automotive-sector-deal-single-pages.pdf

Kilson, K. (2016). *In 1910, electric cars were the best vehicles on the road. What happened?* 4 January. Retrieved from https://www.inverse.com/article/9793-null

KPMG. (2017). *Global automotive executive survey 2017.* Retrieved from https://assets.kpmg.com/content/dam/kpmg/xx/pdf/2017/01/global-automotive-executive-survey-2017.pdf

Kröger, F. (2016). Automated driving in its social, historical and cultural contexts. In M. Maurer, J. C. Gerdes, B. Lenz, & H. Winner (Eds.), *Autonomous driving technical, legal and social aspects* (pp. 41–68). Berlin: Springer.

Le Petit, Y. (2017). *How will electric vehicle transition impact EU jobs?* Retrieved from https://www.transportenvironment.org/sites/te/files/publications/Briefing%20-%20How%20will%20electric%20vehicle%20transition%20impact%20EU%20jobs.pdf

Litman, T. (2018). *Autonomous vehicle implementation predictions: implications for transport planning.* Retrieved from Australia: https://www.vtpi.org/avip.pdf

Loveday, S. (2018). How close are we to a self-driving car? *US News and World Report.* Retrieved from https://cars.usnews.com/cars-trucks/autonomous-vehicle-levels

Melosi, M. V. (2010). *The automobile and the environment in American history.* Retrieved from http://www.autolife.umd.umich.edu/Environment/E_Overview/E_Overview3.htm

PBS. (2009). *Timeline: history of the electric car.* 30 October. Retrieved from http://www.pbs.org/now/shows/223/electric-car-timeline.html

Ray, R. (2016). *Where did the word 'car' for automobiles originate?* 16 October. Retrieved from https://www.quora.com/Where-did-the-word-car-for-automobiles-originate

Sugg, E. G. B. (2018). *Letter to the House of Lords.* London: UK Parliament. Retrieved from http://data.parliament.uk/DepositedPapers/files/DEP2018-0254/Letter_from_Baroness_Sugg_Automated_and_Electric_Vehicles_Bill.pdf

The Irish News. (2018). *Sapiens author Yuval Noah Harari says Brexit is a 'distraction' and a 'fantasy'.* 27 September. Retrieved from https://www.irishnews.com/magazine/entertainment/2018/09/27/news/sapiens-author-yuval-noah-harari-says-brexit-is-a-distraction-and-a-fantasy--1444094/

Thomson, J. J. (1985). The trolley problem. (ethics of killing and letting die). *Yale Law Journal, 94*(6), 1395–1415. doi:10.2307/796133

UK Department of Business Industry & Industrial Strategy. (2018). *Future of mobility.* London: gov.uk. Retrieved from https://www.gov.uk/government/publications/industrial-strategy-the-grand-challenges/missions#zero-emissions

Disruptors 117

UK Government. (1988). *UK Road Traffic Act 1988*. London. Retrieved from https://www.legislation.gov.uk/ukpga/1988/52/contents

UNECE. (2002). *ECE standardization list*. New York/Geneva: The United Nations Economic Commission for Europe. Retrieved from http://unpan1.un.org/intradoc/groups/public/documents/unece/unpan019895.pdf

Union of Concerned Scientists. (2017). *Maximizing the benefits of self-driving vehicles*. Retrieved from https://www.ucsusa.org/clean-vehicles/principles-self-driving-cars#.W5wq-S2ZOi4

van Wyk, R. J. (1987). Innovation: the attacker's advantage. *Futures, 19*(3), 347–349. Retrieved from https://ac-els-cdn-com.ezproxy01.rhul.ac.uk/00163 28787900279/1-s2.0-0016328787900279-main.pdf?_tid=f416b6b1-8ad6-4362-8e41-35546675be18&acdnat=1548628225_d1b5b7dddf41c50568906c5 705642f24. doi:10.1016/0016–3287(87)90027-9

Vanderbilt, T. (2018). Takin it to the streets. *Smithsonian*. Retrieved from https://www.pressreader.com/usa/smithsonian-magazine/20181201/2815 35112004723

Vincent, J. (2017). *DeepMind's Go-playing AI doesn't need human help to beat us anymore*. 18 October. Retrieved from https://www.theverge.com/2017/ 10/18/16495548/deepmind-ai-go-alphago-zero-self-taught

9   The role of cities

The majority in favour of leaving the EU in the UK's referendum was small. The overall result was 17.4 million votes in favour of leave, and 16.1 million for remain, representing a 51.9%/48.1% split. This result was made up of a broad range of results across the UK, with most famously Scotland and Northern Ireland voting to remain in the EU by 62.0%/38.0% and 55.8%/44.2%, respectively (BBC News, 2016). There has been much comment on the ability of the UK to hold together as a State, specifically with moves to Scottish independence and with difficulties of reconciling the ending of the relationship with the EU with maintaining the Good Friday Agreement securing peace and devolved government in Northern Ireland. So, it is quite possible that the positions agreed by the UK government for the UK's new relationship with the EU, if a final position is ever reached, will be subject to continued stress affecting the coherence of the UK. It may not be possible to find a new relationship between the UK and the EU that treats the UK as a single uniform entity, and even if such a position is found it is quite hard to see how it will be sustained. The UK itself will change, and it may well fragment.

London is not seen as a self-governing region within the UK but it has distinct localised decision-making structures that operate across the metropolis and the local government boroughs. London is by some margin the largest city in the EU and while this great metropolis to some extent typifies the UK, it also sits uncomfortably within it by reason of its scale, its diversity and its bankers. According to some commentators, alienation from London may have underpinned majorities for leaving the EU:

> There is a widespread view in the land beyond the M25 that the capital has been the driving force behind a globalising agenda that pays no regard to the customs and way of life of non-metropolitan Britain. London's overwhelming vote to remain will simply be seen as evidence of how out of touch it has become.
>
> (Easton, 2016)

The role of cities   119

This chapter considers how the regulatory process is becoming complicated by the rise of cities such as London which introduce rules at variance with the national standards – be they licensing regulations or restrictions on vehicle use. It summarises the evolving regulatory regime applicable in various cities generally requiring less polluting emissions and the different rules being considered for autonomous vehicles. It argues that the result is a complex patchwork of rules relating to vehicle use which will increasingly make national-level policies relating to vehicles problematic.

Regulatory fragmentation affecting the motor industry

In addition to all the regulatory activity at the national and supra-national levels, large urban areas remain polluted, and unhappy with the pace of national-level actions. As a consequence, one of the significant developments in vehicle emissions in the past few years has been an increase in regulations imposed by sub-national areas. In the US, California has long followed an independent path in emissions standards, always implementing stricter rules than federal requirements. Recently, Paris, London and Seoul frustrated with the pace of environmental actions, announced a programme to 'grade' vehicle emissions in 'real-life' conditions to increase the information available to consumers about the extent to which their vehicles pollute. In a joint announcement in March 2017 the mayors, including London Mayor Sadiq Khan, were explicit; they intend that their metropolises will push vehicle manufacturers to make vehicles cleaner more rapidly (AP, 2017). These actions will add to regulations like congestion charges that already exist. The announcements are important as these mega-cities represent large vehicle markets, and manufacturers want to avoid the cost of producing different versions for different markets. At the December 2017 Paris conference, the Governor of California, Jerry Brown said, "the effort in the US to fight climate change was being led from the cities, from the states" (Breeden & Peltier, 2017). Thus, depending on the extent of the requirements imposed by municipal officials, bespoke urban initiatives may well drive vehicle changes more generally, and limit the impact of national governments.

The rise of municipal regulations

The current concept of nations that impose regulations and define the basis of trade is actually a concept that is only about 400 years old. It evolved during the Renaissance in Europe emerging out of the decline of feudal lords and the Catholic Church (Bowen, 2018). In fact,

120 *The role of cities*

cities long preceded nations as spheres of influence, promoters of trade and centres of commerce. There was an Alexandria long before there was an Egypt, and Rome is far older than Italy (Fullerton, 2017). And while nations may have subsumed much of the power of municipalities, the city has remained a force, and there is evidence that municipalities are retaking some power from central governments by acting unilaterally in their own perceived best interests. The reason for this is the overwhelming size and economic strength of cities. According to the UN about 54% of the world's population today lives in urban areas and this will grow to more than two-thirds by 2050 (United Nations, 2018).[1] While the definition of urban is somewhat vague, McKinsey & Co. estimates that the world's 600 largest cities represent 22% of the global population and more than half of its total GDP. Their survey sample represents centres with populations greater than 150,000 including 23 megacities with populations above 10 million. By 2025 the estimate is that these 600 municipalities will account for 25% of the population and 60% of the GDP (Dobbs et al., 2011).

Increasingly, researchers are arguing that nations are failing to meet the challenges of a globalising world, and cities may be the best hope for success in an interconnected global economy. The fact is that many of the major issues the world faces are urban, and national governments are often gridlocked in arriving at solutions that do not matter to the parts of their population that do not live in cities. In particular, for the future of the motor vehicle industry, most cities are on coastlines or rivers meaning that climate change will have great impact on these areas (Fullerton, 2017). Cities tend to be more pragmatic than national governments and are increasingly distancing themselves from national politics. In 2012 the then mayor of New York, Michael Bloomberg, boasted: "I have my own army in the NYPD, which is the seventh biggest army in the world…I don't listen to Washington very much" (Jelier, 2015). Given that many of the current issues relating to motor vehicles impact cities it is not surprising that they are beginning to operate independently of national governments, and this is only likely to increase as the size and influence of cities grows.

Cities are already beginning to plot independent regulatory courses. Sometimes these are coordinated with national plans, but often they are independent responses to the specific problems metropolitan areas confront. Table 9.1 summarises regulations that some cities are currently pursuing or have already implemented.

These regulations relate to pollution and the congestion that generates it. Vehicle manufacturers are impacted because, for example, banning diesel cars from major areas that are responsible for a large

Table 9.1 Selected city implemented vehicle restrictions

City	Actual/proposed regulation
Athens, Greece	• Diesel vehicles banned from city centre on certain days based on license plate numbers • All diesel cars banned from 2025
Beijing, China	• Those wishing to purchase an internal-combustion engine car must enter a lottery and can wait two years to receive a license plate. State-approved electric vehicles receive licenses more easily
Berlin, Germany	• Low emission zone banning all diesel vehicles and petrol vehicles failing emission standards • Planning new bike superhighway separated from cars and pedestrians
Bogotá, Colombia	• 75 miles of roads prohibit vehicles one day every week • License plate restrictions • 200 miles of bicycle-only lanes
Brussels, Belgium	• Car-free Sundays • Selected streets converted to pedestrian areas • Diesel cars built before 1998 banned • Public transport will be free on high air pollution days
Chengdu, China	• New residential areas designed so that residents can walk anywhere in 15 minutes • Only half the roads planned to allow vehicles by 2020
Copenhagen, Denmark	• Pledging to become carbon neutral by 2025; over half the population bikes to work • 28 planned bike superhighways to surrounding suburbs • Diesel car ban proposed by 2019
Hamburg, Germany	• Older diesel cars banned • Car-free "green-network" planned to cover 40% of the urban area by 2035
Helsinki, Finland	• No direct ban on cars, but creating incentives to make alternative transportation so good that no one will have reason to own a car
London, England	• Diesel cars banned from 2020 • Most polluting cars pay a fee (T-charge) in central London • Ultra Low Emission Zone (ULEZ) proposal from 2019 enacting the "toughest emission standard of any world city" according to Mayor Sadiq Khan
Madrid, Spain	• From November, 2018 non-resident vehicles banned in the city centre • Cars banned from 500 acres of city centre by 2020 • Heavy polluting vehicles will pay more to park • Pedestrian only zones created

(Continued)

122 *The role of cities*

City	Actual/proposed regulation
Mexico City, Mexico	• Road use restricted by license plate number
Milan, Italy	• Most polluting cars banned from the city centre • Public transportation vouchers for commuters who leave their vehicles home
New York City, USA	• Times square revamped as pedestrian zone • Additional streets proposed to become car-free
Oslo, Norway	• All private vehicles banned by 2019 (six years before a country-wide ban) • Replacing 35 miles of roads with bike lanes • Congestion fees and potential rush hour charges • 2019 ban on parking spaces
Paris, France	• Vehicles built before 1997 banned from entering the city on weekdays • Champs-Élysées closes once a month to traffic • 1.8-mile section of the Seine right bank pedestrianised • Diesel vehicles banned from 2025 • Select streets only open to electric vehicles by 2020
Seoul, South Korea	• Diesel vehicles failing emissions standards banned
Tokyo, Japan	• Since 2000, diesel vehicles banned except those with installed exhaust-fume purifiers

Sources: Barber, 2018; Garfield, 2018; McKinsey, 2013.

number of vehicle sales makes those vehicles less profitable, and encourages manufacturers to move to other products. The September 2018 announcement by Porsche that it was dropping diesel cars may be an example. While VW, the parent company of Porsche, did much on its own to damage the reputation of diesel vehicles by being caught installing emissions-testing software, the chief executive of Porsche, Oliver Blume, insisted the decision was "not demonising diesel", but that "We as a sports car manufacturer...have come to the conclusion that we would like our future to be diesel-free" (BBC, 2018). One suspects that the fact that these products would no longer be able to enter some of the largest cities in the world was at least a consideration in the decision process.

Not surprisingly cities are only beginning to consider how they will deal with autonomous vehicles since these cars are in an early stage of the innovation curve and only beginning to be tested. In the case of the US, where the federal government is always a follower in the regulatory environment, and at present has a strongly anti-regulation administration, it is the states that have begun to consider how and whether autonomous vehicles should be regulated. Even prior to the

The role of cities 123

Trump administration, the US National Highway Traffic Safety Administration (NHTSA) prepared guidelines for states that are considering autonomous vehicle regulations essentially pleading with them to not go off on their own. The 2016 Federal Automated Vehicles Policy argued

> Today, a motorist can drive across state lines without a worry more complicated than, "did the speed limit change?" The integration of (automated vehicles) should not change that ability. Similarly, a manufacturer should be able to focus on developing a single HAV fleet rather than 50 different versions to meet individual state requirements.
>
> (NHTSA, 2016, p. 7)

However, the traditional fear of treading too heavily on the states leads the report to stress: "This guidance is not mandatory" (NHTSA, 2016, p. 11). Accordingly, the states are doing their own thing with 27 of them having now enacted some form of regulation controlling autonomous vehicles (NCSL, 2018). It is only a matter of time before the larger cities consider their own rules.

The rules being enacted by US states consider a wide variety of issues as they apply to AVs:

- Commercial sales
- Cybersecurity
- Defining AVs
- Infrastructure
- Insurance and liability
- Licensing and registration
- Operation on public roads
- Operator requirements
- Privacy of collected data
- Inspections
- Testing

It is likely that a subset of these individual legislated provisions will condense into a single framework, but however that structure evolves, manufacturers will be obliged to comply. The disparity of vehicle regulations between Europe and the US has always been an inhibitor for vehicle trade where manufacturers had to accept the cost of compliance. The situation will be the same for autonomous vehicles, and a post-Brexit Britain will not have much influence on the outcome.

124 *The role of cities*

As cities begin to consider the implications for autonomous vehicles, it is likely that their interests will be different than national or state rules regarding licensing, safety and liability. Cities are beginning to concentrate on their liveability and community. They will be intently focused on the safety of their residents, the potential to reduce congestion and the use of space in ways to improve their overall environment. As cities rapidly expand, planners who are thinking about the future of a metropolitan world are studying many changes to managing growth, and among those considerations is how autonomous vehicles operate. In a recent lecture, the architect Vishaan Chakrabarti argued that the rapid growth in cities requires society to rethink urban design because "how we design those urban areas could well determine whether we thrive or not as a species" (Chakrabarti, 2018). Specifically, for autonomous vehicles he stated:

> I don't think the autonomous vehicle is exciting because it's a driverless car. That, to me, only implies that there's even more congestion on the roads, frankly. I think what's exciting about the autonomous vehicle is the promise...that we could have these small, urban vehicles that could safely comingle with pedestrians and bicycles.
>
> (Chakrabarti, 2018)

It is likely that the largest cities of the world, and those that are moving towards that designation, will insist autonomous vehicles be something that enhances quality of life in their environments, which may well lead to regulations relating to size, usage, parking and communication as well as areas where they can be driven. It is probable that the autonomous vehicle, at least as it is used in the largest cities will be forced to combine with electric powertrains, which given the importance of large populations to vehicle sales, will determine the future of both autonomous and electric transportation modes. The outcome of all of the uncertainty surrounding autonomous vehicles is difficult to predict, because as one analyst put it simply – "the future is messy" (Marshall, 2017). How a UK vehicle industry untethered from the EU effectively participates in that mess seems problematic.

Note

1 The UN does not have a definition of urban population; they use the data as reported by each country.

References

AP. (2017). *Paris, London, Seoul to 'grade' cars based on emissions.* Retrieved from http://www.businessinsider.com/ap-paris-london-seoul-to-grade-cars-based-on-emissions-2017-3

Barber, M. (2018). *15 cities tackling pollution by curbing cars.* 14 August. Retrieved from https://www.curbed.com/2017/4/10/15207926/car-ban-cities-pollution-traffic-paris-london-mexico-city

BBC. (2018). *Porsche stops making diesel cars after VW emissions scandal.* 23 September. Retrieved from https://www.bbc.com/news/world-europe-45619994

BBC News. (2016). UK votes to leave the EU. *BBC News.* Retrieved from https://www.bbc.com/news/politics/eu_referendum/results

Bowen, W. R. (2018). *The Rise of the Nation-State.* Retrieved from https://owlcation.com/humanities/nation-state

Breeden, A., & Peltier, E. (2017). Macron holds a climate summit, and Trump casts a shadow. *New York Times.* Retrieved from https://www.nytimes.com/2017/12/12/world/europe/macron-climate-summit.html?rref=collection%2Ftimestopic%2FGreenhouse%20Gas%20Emissions&action=click&contentCollection=timestopics&region=stream&module=stream_unit&version=latest&contentPlacement=6&pgtype=collection

Chakrabarti, V. (Producer). (2018). *How can we design timeless cities for our collective future.* Retrieved from https://www.ted.com/talks/vishaan_chakrabarti_how_we_can_design_timeless_cities_for_our_collective_future/transcript#t-812072

Dobbs, R., Smit, S., Remes, J., Manyika, J., Roxburgh, C., & Restrepo, A. (2011). *Urban world: mapping the economic power of cities.* Retrieved from https://www.mckinsey.com/~/media/McKinsey/Featured%20Insights/Urbanization/Urban%20world/MGI_urban_world_mapping_economic_power_of_cities_full_report.ashx

Easton, M. (2016). A less than United Kingdom. *BBC News.* Retrieved from https://www.bbc.com/news/uk-politics-eu-referendum-36605656

Fullerton, J. (2017). City States Rising! 2 January. Retrieved from https://www.huffingtonpost.com/john-fullerton/city-states-rising_b_13932212.html

Garfield, L. (2018). *13 cities that are starting to ban cars.* 1 January. Retrieved from https://www.businessinsider.com/cities-going-car-free-ban-2017-8#oslo-norway-will-implement-its-car-ban-by-2019-1

Jelier, R. (2015). The Rising Metropolis: Mayors and Cities leading the way— But is it revolutionary? *Public Administration Review, 76*(1), 7. Retrieved from https://onlinelibrary.wiley.com/doi/abs/10.1111/puar.12496. doi:10.1111/puar.12496

Marshall, A. (2017). *Robocars could add $7 trillion to the global economy.* 3 June. Retrieved from https://www.wired.com/2017/06/impact-of-autonomous-vehicles/

126 The role of cities

McKinsey. (2013). *The road to 2020 and beyond: what's driving the global automotive industry?* Retrieved from https://www.mckinsey.com/~/media/mckinsey/dotcom/client_service/Automotive%20and%20Assembly/PDFs/McK_The_road_to_2020_and_beyond.ashx

NCSL. (2018). *Self-driving vehicles enacted legislation.* National Conference of State Legislatures. Retrieved from http://www.ncsl.org/research/transportation/autonomous-vehicles-self-driving-vehicles-enacted-legislation.aspx#Enacted%20Autonomous%20Vehicle%20Legislation

NHTSA. (2016). *Federal automated vehicles policy.* Washington, DC. Retrieved from https://www.transportation.gov/AV/federal-automated-vehicles-policy-september-2016

United Nations. (2018). *World Urbanization Prospects: the 2018 revision.* United Nations Population Division, Department of Economic and Social Affairs. Retrieved from https://www.un.org/development/desa/publications/2018-revision-of-world-urbanization-prospects.html

10 What if it gets ugly?

Of all the potential outcomes of the Brexit process, the one certainty is that not everything will be resolved on the date the UK formally leaves the European Union. The debate in the UK since the referendum result, and following the Prime Minister's letter setting out notification of departure under Article 50 of the Treaty of European Union has been protracted and divisive, but that debate has been about the terms of the UK's departure. The future relationship is at best sketchily mapped out in the withdrawal proposal. Even assuming Brexit happens, there will be ongoing debate about the new forms of cooperation needed to trade and to deal with other matters, such as security.

At the time of this writing there is no agreement on future relations between the EU and the UK, the withdrawal agreement was rejected multiple times by Parliament, the 29 March deadline has passed and the timeline for a decision has been kicked down the road until the end of October 2019. A lot of commentary is focussed on what may happen in the event of a departure without a deal between the UK and the EU. While that is one risk, the question of a no deal departure is only one scenario. The same economic problems could arise from a bad deal or a poorly managed departure. This chapter reviews the potential impact of a bad departure – either without a deal or with a bad deal – on the UK car industry. It argues that the impact could well lead to the ending of vehicle manufacturing in the UK, but while this may seem to be a prediction laden with doom, in fact many countries manage quite well without a vehicle industry and there are examples of societies which have successfully transitioned from having vehicle industries to having no such industry.

As argued earlier, there are industries other than motor vehicle manufacturing that are at risk and have potentially a greater impact on the UK economic future than the motor industry. That risk has been highlighted by a January 2019 CNN report that banks and other

128 *What if it gets ugly?*

financial companies have already shifted £800 billion from the UK because of Brexit risks (Kottasová, 2019). However, it is useful to consider the worst-case scenario – what might happen if car manufacturing ceased in the UK? Countries that have lost vehicle manufacturing provide a useful insight. Some, like Venezuela, lost assembly due to economic collapse, but most have fallen victim to the same global economic forces that confront the UK – required volume for economies of scale, global logistics and consumer demand for the lowest cost cars. Three relatively recent examples worth examining are Australia, New Zealand and California.

Australia assembly cessation

Australia had a long history of vehicle manufacturing stretching back to the first steam car built in 1896 (Eisenstein, 2017). Being geographically isolated, in the early part of the 20th century the country developed its own locally made cars. Vehicles from various sources were also assembled using imported components, however in August 1917, at the start of World War I, the government banned the importation of luxury goods which included car bodies (Florance & Best, 2018). Thus, the industry evolved with high local content. Two corporations that would dominate Australian vehicle manufacturing for most of the 20th century, Ford and Holden (a subsidiary of General Motors), began assembly in 1925 and 1931, respectively (Florance & Best, 2018). At its peak in 1974 Australian assembly approached 475,000 vehicles (Eisenstein, 2017).

When the government relaxed import restrictions, maintaining local manufacturing required significant government support to enable local products to compete against low-cost imports. In the mid-1980s the government decided to pull the plug; the industry lost tariff protection but maintained a series of expensive subsidies (FCAI, 2009). Between 1997 and 2012, Australian taxpayers spent A\$30 billion on subsidies to support local vehicle manufacturing (Barclay, 2017). Events came to a head in 2013 when Ford announced the closure of its plants, and the government aggressively attacked Holden demanding to know what its plans were. Shortly thereafter Holden announced it would close followed by Toyota (Australian Broadcasting Corporation, 2014; Hawthorne, 2014).

The announcements led to the usual criticisms about the impact on workers and the economy, combined with arguments that the closures could lead to the loss of strategic manufacturing skills and harm national security (Worrall & Spoehr, 2014, p. 6). There were pronouncements that the loss of vehicle manufacturing would cost 200,000 jobs and lead to a reduction of GDP by 2% (Westbrook, 2017). The last vehicle manufacturing plant closed in 2017, so it is still too early to assess the ultimate impact of the cessation of local vehicle manufacturing. However, it is worth noting that for the year ending in June 2018 Australia's real GDP grew by 2.8%, equal to or greater than all but two years in the previous ten, and the IMF projects Australia's real GDP for all of 2018 to grow 3.2%. The IMF also projects that Australia's real GDP will continue to grow through 2023 by rates that exceed virtually any other advanced economy (Australian Bureau of Statistics, 2018; IMF, 2018, p. 172). Clearly there are many elements that impact GDP, and the global economy has been strong, but the worst fears have so far not occurred (Trading Economics, 2018).

While it is difficult to make precise comparisons to the UK, the vehicle manufacturing industry contributed about 1% of Australia's GDP, similar to 0.9% currently in the UK (FCAI, 2009; ONS, 2018). In addition, while manufacturing has ended there remains a lot that vehicles contribute to the Australian economy. The Victorian Automobile Chamber of Commerce estimates that through such businesses as retailing, repairing, maintaining, rental and towing the automotive industry will continue to contribute 2.1% of Australia's GDP, down only a tenth of a point from when vehicle and component manufacturing existed (VACC, 2017, p. 17). This may be optimistic forecasting on the part of an industry association, but it does indicate the importance of the residual portions of the country's motor industry. Vehicles will still be sold and driven. It has also been noted as another benefit that from the policy changes Australians have some of the lowest prices for vehicles in the world (Barclay, 2017).

End of New Zealand assembly

The case of New Zealand provides more historical context of the end of vehicle assembly. Assembly operations in New Zealand were different from UK manufacturing, in that cars were built from imported kits in low volume in a process known as Completely Knocked Down (CKD). Beginning in 1926 and for more than 75 years the government discouraged imports of built up cars through high tariffs, local content requirements and licensing (TEARA, 2018). In 1966, near the peak of local assembly, there were 17 automotive plants producing fewer than 59,000 units, an average of only about 3,500 per plant (World Bank, 1966). Despite the small scale, CKD assembly is highly labour intensive, so in that same year auto assembly and related industries represented more than 9% of total employment in the country. Thus, it was an important industry.

130 *What if it gets ugly?*

The government decided to lift import restrictions in 1972 which prophesied the end of local manufacturing. In the 1980s tariffs were reduced further accelerating the decline of local production. The final three Japanese-owned assemblers closed in 1998, the year vehicle tariffs were eliminated. Despite the closures, the impact of the death of this industry on the New Zealand economy was not a disaster. Figure 10.1 shows the New Zealand GDP growth between 1990 and 2008 prior to and after the end of vehicle assembly.

Again, GDP growth is dependent on a lot of factors, and New Zealand's GDP, as a relatively small economy, tends to be volatile. But following the closure of car assembly the economy performed no worse than it had in the decade before the termination. The economy survived the loss of its motor vehicle industry. This is not a new argument. Well before the Brexit vote, in testimony to the House of Commons Foreign Affairs Committee, Professor Patrick Minford of Cardiff University stated that "It is perfectly true that if you remove protection of the sort that has been given particularly to the car industry…you are going to have to run it down" (House of Commons, 2012). Far from being negative about that eventuality, however, Minford argued that the benefits of free trade will more than offset the loss and that running down the car industry "will be in your interests to do it, just as in the same way we ran down the coal and steel industries" (House of Commons, 2012). Obviously, there are those in the involved industries who would argue that point, but the experiences in other countries suggest the loss would not be economically devastating.

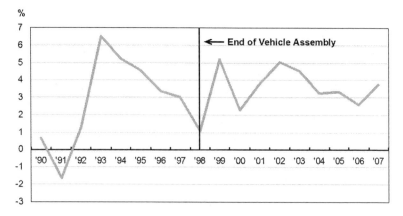

Figure 10.1 NZ GDP annual percent change.
Source: New Zealand Statistics Archive (Government of New Zealand, 2018).

California

If taken as a stand-alone economy, California recently moved into fifth place globally. This is ahead of the UK which has been struggling lately (Fuller, 2018). As a retail market for vehicles California is close to the UK with 2.1 million vehicles sold in 2017 compared to 2.5 million in the UK (Nikolewski, 2018; SMMT, 2018). At the end of World War II California had significant vehicle manufacturing. Over time, however, plants closed and today, other than some component part manufacturing, the only assembled vehicles are Teslas that are built in a former General Motors plant in Fremont. That plant assembles only about 100,000 vehicles per year, so effectively vehicle assembly no longer exists in California (Estrada, 2018). Yet, the California economy continues to flourish having recovered well from the financial crisis. No one seems concerned that vehicle manufacturing has largely departed.

The lesson from the above examples is that while the future of UK vehicle assembly does not look promising in the longer term, Brexit or not, the UK economy will survive the loss of this manufacturing. There are in fact areas of vehicle development that may well be suited to the expertise the UK has in research and computerisation that can continue a UK role in the next phase of this industry. But, there is scepticism about the future of the auto industry in the UK. In reviewing the possible threat of electric vehicles to traditional manufacturing, a Bloomberg analyst compared this risk to the immediate job cutting that is occurring, which is at least partly the result of Brexit uncertainty, and concluded: "Technological change is a reasonable cause of job losses; political self-harm is not" (Bryant, 2019).

References

Australian Broadcasting Corporation. (2014). *Holden announces October deadline for end of Australian car production.* 13 January Updated 13 January 2017. Retrieved from http://www.abc.net.au/news/2017-01-13/holden-announces-october-closure-date/8181144

Australian Bureau of Statistics. (2018). *Australian system of national accounts: Table 1. key national accounts aggregates.* Canberra. Retrieved from https://www.abs.gov.au/AUSSTATS/abs@.nsf/DetailsPage/5204.02017-18?OpenDocument

Barclay, A. (2017). *This is the last year a car will be made in Australia.* 25 April. Retrieved from https://qz.com/967631/as-general-motors-gm-closes-its-holden-factory-this-is-the-last-year-a-car-will-be-made-in-australia/

Bryant, C. (2019). Where Ford and Jaguar Lead, the Rest Will Surely Follow: The carmakers are struggling with the epochal change to electric motors. Expect

132 *What if it gets ugly?*

thousands more job losses in the next decade. *bloomberg.com*. Retrieved from https://www.bloomberg.com/opinion/articles/2019-01-10/ford-and-jaguar-land-rover-job-cuts-are-just-the-start

Eisenstein, P. A. (2017). *Australia's 100-Year-Old Automobile Industry Just Closed Down*. 20 October. Retrieved from https://www.nbcnews.com/business/autos/australia-s-100-year-old-automobile-industry-just-closed-down-n812756

Estrada, Z. (2018). *Tesla reports best year ever for deliveries, but falls further behind on Model 3 goals*. 3 January. Retrieved from https://www.theverge.com/2018/1/3/16846860/tesla-2017-deliveries-model-3-production

FCAI. (2009). *Submission to the inquiry into manufacturing in Victoria*. Federal Chamber of *Automotive Industries*. Retrieved from https://www.parliament.vic.gov.au/images/stories/committees/edic/submissions/VMI_Sub_58_FCAI.pdf

Florance, L., & Best, C. (2018). *Ford Australia ceases production: timeline of the company's decades-long history in the country*. 22 February. Retrieved from http://www.abc.net.au/news/2016-10-07/timeline-ford-australia-ceases-production/7911742

Fuller, T. (2018). The Pleasure and Pain of Being California, the World's 5th-Largest Economy. *New York Times*. Retrieved from https://www.nytimes.com/2018/05/07/us/california-economy-growth.html

Government of New Zealand. (2018). *New Zealand statistics archive*. Retrieved from http://archive.stats.govt.nz/infoshare/ViewTable.aspx?pxID=855603db-b349-4aa1-8ed9-12e895e73175

Hawthorne, M. (2014). Toyota to exit Australia, 30,000 jobs could go. *The Sydney Morning Herald*. Retrieved from https://www.smh.com.au/business/toyota-to-exit-australia-30000-jobs-could-go-20140210-32cl3.html

House of Commons. (2012). *The future of the European Union: UK government policy*. London: UK Parliament. Retrieved from https://publications.parliament.uk/pa/cm201213/cmselect/cmfaff/c115-iii/c11501.htm

IMF. (2018). *World Economic Outlook: Challenges to Steady Growth*. Washington, DC, October. Retrieved from https://www.imf.org/~/media/Files/Publications/WEO/2018/October/English/main-report/Text.ashx

Kottasová, I. (2019). $1 trillion is leaving Britain because of Brexit. *CNN.com*. Retrieved from https://www.cnn.com/2019/01/07/investing/brexit-banks-moving-assets/index.html

Nikolewski, R. (2018). California vehicle sales exceed 2 million for third straight year. *San Diego Union-Tribune*. Retrieved from https://www.sandiegouniontribune.com/business/energy-green/sd-fi-car-sales-20180222-story.html

ONS. (2018). *Gross Domestic Product*. Retrieved from: https://www.ons.gov.uk/economy/grossdomesticproductgdp/datasets/ukgdpolowlevelaggregates

SMMT. (2018). *Motor industry facts 2018*. Retrieved from https://www.smmt.co.uk/reports/smmt-motor-industry-facts-2018/

TEARA. (2018). *Demise of the car-assembly and component industries*. Retrieved from https://teara.govt.nz/en/cars-and-the-motor-industry/page-4

Trading Economics. (2018). *Australia GDP Annual Growth Rate.* Retrieved from https://d3fy65lgv2fhd3.cloudfront.net/charts/australia-gdp-growth-annual.png?s=aunagdpy&v=201809061337x

VACC. (2017). *Directions in Australia's automotive industry: an industry report 2017.* Retrieved from Melbourne: http://www.mtaa.com.au/images/docs/Directions_in_Australias_Automotive_Industry.pdf

Westbrook, J. T. (2017). *The Death Of Australia's Automotive Industry Was A 30-Year Plot To Avoid Economic Collapse.* 26 April. Retrieved from https://jalopnik.com/the-death-of-australias-automotive-industry-was-a-30-ye-1794688752

World Bank. (1966). *New Zealand national statistics.* Retrieved from http://documents.worldbank.org/curated/en/405991468054624102/text/multi-0page.txt

Worrall, L., & Spoehr, J. (2014). *The future of the automotive transformation scheme: submission to senate standing committee on economics.* Retrieved from http://www.flinders.edu.au/fms/AITI/Documents/wiser201450_future_of_automotive_transformation_scheme.pdf

11 Final thoughts

This book has attempted to increase the understanding of the vehicle industry in the UK and the impact on the industry and the UK economy as a result of Brexit. In addition, we have examined regulation versus market forces in the vehicle industry to contemplate how the industry may need to respond in the face of the significant changes that are occurring to vehicles globally regardless of whether there is Brexit or not. In the course of this investigation we have noted that although the motor industry is significant, it is not of the magnitude of other industries, and in the scheme of businesses that may be harmed by Brexit, the motor industry seems to garner more than its share of concern. We conclude that Brexit is a threat to UK vehicle assembly, but that car manufacturing jobs will be under duress anyway as electric and autonomous vehicles emerge in large volumes.

The UK government's own industrial strategy for the automotive industry acknowledges that "In the next ten years, the sector will see more change than in the previous hundred" (HM Government, 2018). The industry will transition away from the complicated assembly required for internal combustion vehicles, and the focus will transition to batteries and sophisticated electronics. There certainly will be opportunities for the UK in this transition, but the days of labour-intensive vehicle assembly are going to diminish regardless of the outcome of Brexit. The era of a stand-alone vehicle industry where the UK follows its own path has ended. The vehicle industry, similar to many industries, is international in its composition. In terms of the UK's ability to escape the restrictions of EU regulations, and through this freedom to increase innovation, economic growth and opportunities, we conclude that Brexit is unlikely to benefit the motor industry.

As an example of the UK's loss of influence in a post-Brexit environment, consider the current situation related to vehicle safety regulations. In May 2018 the European Commission adopted a proposal

Final thoughts 135

for additional vehicle safety requirements. This proposal is referred to by the Commission as a "paradigm shift in standard vehicle safety equipment" (European Commission, 2018). The proposed regulations cover a wide array of car requirements such as child restraint systems, proposals to protect pedestrians and cyclists as well as accident avoidance measures covering emergency braking and lane keeping systems. In addition, there is a proposal to install an emergency call system in vehicles to shorten the time it takes for emergency services to arrive in the event of an accident. There are also proposals to reduce blind spots for lorries. Significantly, one of the proposals would change the testing procedure to verify compliance. Some of these requirements will be controversial as they will increase vehicle production costs, but the UK will have no input into the decisions, and while the original Government White Paper indicated the EU would accept UK type approval results, the UK will be forced to modify its testing procedures to match whatever the EU approves in order to be able to sell into the continent (UK Parliament, 2018, p. 21).

It is also true that if the UK is to develop independent trade relationships with other countries, the products they sell must conform to the regulations in force in those countries. In the US, those are the Federal Motor Vehicle Safety Standards (FMVSS), the national programme for greenhouse gas emissions (GHG) and fuel economy standards developed jointly by the US Environmental Protection Agency (EPA) and the National Highway Traffic Safety Administration (NHTSA). In the EU, the requirements are the extensive set of safety and environmental regulations that form the basis for the United Nations World Forum for the harmonisation of vehicle regulations (WP.29) which are formally accepted by more than 60 countries that represent most of the largest vehicle markets and recognised by many others. Unless the UK conforms to one or the other or both of these codes it will not export vehicles. The UK being outside of the EU means that it will have little if any input into future rule updates, and as the global vehicle industry enters a period of substantial change with electric and autonomous vehicles there will be many changes in the regulatory framework. An additional consequence of being outside the EU is that post-Brexit UK electric car production will not count towards EU manufacturers' CO_2 reduction commitments and this will certainly reduce the incentive to locate assembly in the country (Campbell, 2018).

The question becomes where might the UK motor industry go in the future? Certainly, the outcome will have a lot to do with how Brexit evolves. If the UK reaches some agreement with the EU to maintain open borders for goods and services the industry may continue much

136 *Final thoughts*

as it is but will be required to match any standards changes the EU implements. If, however, it turns out that there is any increase in border controls between the UK and the EU for goods and services, the cost of vehicle manufacturing in the UK will rise, and unless declines in the pound offset those losses, vehicle manufacturers will eventually decide to consolidate assembly elsewhere. We believe it unlikely that the UK government would begin a major programme of subsidies to offset the industry loses. This transition will likely occur over a period of years as a given manufacturer reaches a new model introduction break point. The UK may have a long history of vehicle manufacturing tradition, but so did Australia and New Zealand.

The government does recognise the challenges. In its 2018 Automotive Sector Deal, there are proposals to increase support to address the looming issues. The government promises to:

- Invest £500m over ten years to develop new automotive-related technology
- Spend £225m from 2023 to 2026 to support R&D in the sector
- Make the UK a world leader in batteries to support electric vehicles through another £246m in spending
- Invest another £250m to become a leader in autonomous vehicles

In addition, the government is studying the benefits of another £16m in funding to develop an internationally competitive supply chain for future vehicle production. It is positive that the need for these concepts has been identified, however no matter how well intentioned, with more than $80 billion in investments already made by other nations it is unlikely that these actions will result in a sustainable competitive advantage (Loveday, 2018). Government will not be the ultimate answer to moving the UK to the forefront of the transportation future. A more than decade old report by the UK Department of Transportation and Industry got it right when they indicated at that juncture that success will more likely be achieved through a collaborative process between government, academia, small research firms and large corporations (Department of Trade and Industry, 2005).

It is possible that the evolution in transportation systems turns out to be positive. We have described how the loss of vehicle manufacturing in other countries did not destroy their economies; resources shifted in other directions to re-establish growth. If the UK is successful in developing a competitive advantage in electric car and autonomous vehicle technology, there could be big pay-offs even as the number of

Final thoughts 137

manufacturing jobs declines. The benefits to the environment and the freeing of time through reduced traffic congestion may have important positive consequences for society regardless of the manufacturing situation in the vehicle industry. This is, of course, possible whether there is Brexit or not, but the urgency of developing some sustainable advantage would be heightened if manufacturing declines due to border controls on vehicle components. It is unlikely that the AV technology will generate the same number of jobs as a car assembly plant, but the positions that replace those are likely to be high-paying.

It is difficult to forecast how the future changes in transportation will benefit the overall economy, but it is likely to be substantial. As an example, it is estimated that the average Briton spends the equivalent of one working day each week driving. This amounts to three years on the road during a lifetime (Telegraph.co.uk, 2011). The efficiency improvements that may result from automated vehicles would run throughout the economy. A recent study suggested that automated vehicles may lead to a $7 trillion boost to the global economy as "service, application and content revenue generated by mobility-as-a-service will exceed the value of vehicle sales" (Marshall, 2017). This disruption will have winners and losers. The lesson for the UK related to the motor industry is that this disruption will occur regardless of Brexit. Brexit may turn out, at least for the vehicle industry, as a footnote in the tsunami of change. A century ago, few would have forecasted how much the horseless carriage would change the world. It is time for the vehicle industry to look beyond Brexit and develop the potential of the future.

Brexit negotiators unlikely to make optimal choices

The Brexit decision coincides with a dynamic time in the evolving history of vehicle regulations. Requirements and regulators will not cease to exist, but their impact may be overtaken by municipal initiatives, and the market itself. It is difficult to predict what technology, science and politics will prevail. After all, just a decade ago diesel was thought to be the clean fuel answer. Electric vehicles are receiving a lot of attention but suffer from the same issue that have constrained them for a century – the cords are too short, not to mention the environmental challenges of battery recycling. It may be that the most feasible solution will be self-driving vehicles that provide personalised metropolitan transportation with energy efficiency. The fact is that the Brexit and post-Brexit political negotiators will not have sufficient insight to be able to foresee, let alone regulate, optimal solutions.

138 *Final thoughts*

The fact that technological developments are impacting the vehicle industry in ways not seen for a century befogs the Brexit impact. Were there no Brexit to talk about, the UK vehicle manufacturing industry would be under duress if, as seem likely, electric vehicles and autonomous vehicles come to prominence. This will impact not only the UK but also vehicle manufacturing globally. The number of automotive manufacturing jobs overall will surely decline, and this will impact the UK industry. For the next several years, however, were there no Brexit, UK vehicle manufacturing would likely continue as it does currently, because the inertia generated by large plant and equipment investments does not change quickly. But Brexit changes the equation. The industry relies critically on seamless logistics. Even if the Brexit has zero tariffs, but border controls cause delays, such interruptions amount to cost increases the same as a tax. Unless the negotiators miraculously get the EU to agree to a continuation of free movement of goods, the economics of UK vehicle assembly deteriorate quickly. The conclusion is that the UK vehicle manufacturing industry is likely to decline; Brexit only determines the speed at which it decreases.

References

Campbell, P. (2018). No-deal Brexit threatens electric car market. *Financial Times*. Retrieved from https://www.ft.com/content/c45cd3ae-b76a-11e8-bbc3-ccd7de085ffe

Department of Trade and Industry. (2005). *A study of the UK automotive engine industry*. Retrieved from https://www.lowcvp.org.uk/assets/reports/DTI%20Study%20of%20the%20UK%20Automotive%20Engine%20Industry%20-%20June%202005.pdf

European Commission. (2018). *Safety in the automotive sector*. Retrieved from https://ec.europa.eu/growth/sectors/automotive/safety_en

HM Government. (2018). *Industrial strategy: automotive sector deal*. London. Retrieved from https://assets.publishing.service.gov.uk/government/uploads/system/uploads/attachment_data/file/673045/automotive-sector-deal-single-pages.pdf

Loveday, S. (2018). How close are we to a self-driving car? *US News and World Report*. Retrieved from https://cars.usnews.com/cars-trucks/autonomous-vehicle-levels

Marshall, A. (2017). *Robocars could add $7 trillion to the global economy*. 3 June. Retrieved from https://www.wired.com/2017/06/impact-of-autonomous-vehicles/

Telegraph.co.uk. (2011). *Britons spend more time driving than socialising*. Retrieved from https://www.telegraph.co.uk/motoring/news/8287098/Britons-spend-more-time-driving-than-socialising.html

Final thoughts   139

UK Parliament. (2018). *The future relationship between the United Kingdom and the European Union*. London: Presented to Parliament by the Prime Minister by Command of Her Majesty. Retrieved from https://assets.publishing.service.gov.uk/government/uploads/system/uploads/attachment_data/file/725288/The_future_relationship_between_the_United_Kingdom_and_the_European_Union.pdf

Appendix I
Dashboard

The UK's departure from the EU poses numerous industry-specific challenges for motor manufacturing at a time when the industry is going through existential change and simultaneously to accelerating concerns about climate change to which motorised transport contributes significantly.

Red: Urgent issues to resolve

- UK vehicle manufacturing is an assembly operation depending on its supply chain. This supply chain currently depends upon the EU's framework of the free movement of goods.

  - A new framework should replicate the free movement of goods system to enable assembly operation to continue.
  - Any increase in border controls will raise the cost of vehicle manufacturing in the UK.
  - A consistent decline in the value of the pound sterling could offset some losses but given that the majority of vehicle components are imported, declines in sterling will also increase production costs.
  - Cost increases will lead manufacturers to reconsider production locations. With high fixed investment in plant and equipment, those decisions will not happen immediately, but at any break point for new models, cost will be the deciding factor.
  - Domestic components cannot be easily substituted for imported parts.

- Access to the EU market will continue to be a priority whatever the UK's status vis-à-vis EU trading rules.

142 *Appendix I*

- Assuming a trading arrangement with fixed or zero tariffs, the access rules will also entail showing UK cars comply with origin rules, that is, the cars are UK manufactures. UK vehicle exporters will have to attest that they meet an origin requirement set at around 60%.
- Current local value content of UK-produced cars is around 40%.
- Non-native components will likely revert to WTO most favoured nations tariffs.
- Hence, the origin rules will complicate any trading deal on tariffs between the EU and the UK unless UK manufacturers can shift the proportion of the assembly to more UK parts.

- The EU's Whole Vehicle Type Approval (WVTA) regime licences vehicles for sale and use. Benefiting from WVTA currently requires manufacturers to be established in the EU.

  - Changes to the WVTA could be made but a change to achieve WVTA permissions for non-established manufacturers will require some negotiation.
  - Manufacturers' representatives can seek to re-establish within the EU to utilise the EU WVTA.

- Unless the UK conforms to either the US or EU vehicle regulatory codes, it will not export vehicles to most places in the world.

  - Bilateral trade agreements will not alter established requirements.

- Post-Brexit UK electric car production will not count towards EU manufacturers' CO_2 reduction commitments lowering the incentive to locate assembly in the country.

Amber: Minor issues to resolve

- Standards in the motor vehicle industry are led by technical requirements relating to safety and to polluting emissions.

  - Outside the EU, the UK will be free to implement its own regulations, but will still seek to sell vehicles into the EU market. The freedom to set different standards will have little value unless these match EU – or potentially US – requirements.
  - Outside the EU, the UK will have little influence on determining standards in the EU.
  - The EU will continue to control UN regulations which apply to much of the world.

Appendix I 143

- The UK will cease to be an EU approval authority. As a result:
  - The UK will no longer be able to sell vehicles in the EU market with only a certificate of conformity issued by the UK approval authority.
  - Manufacturers will require certification from an EU approved authority.
- Industry disruptors including electric and autonomous vehicles will lead to industrial and regulatory change.
  - Will the UK be willing/able to establish a competitive position?

Green: Staying the same

- Wholesale and retail trade and repair of motor vehicles will be insulated from the Brexit risk, except to the extent that declines in the value of pound sterling increase repair parts prices.
- UN Global Technical Regulations, part of the UN 1998 Agreement, are not mandatory for contracting parties. As a result, UK exports must abide by individual importing country regulations, the same as today.

Index

antilock braking systems (ABS) 89, 90
Aston Martin 24
Australia: loss of vehicle manufacturing 22, 128–9, 136; vehicle definition 99
Automotive Sector Deal 103
autonomous vehicles (AV): development impact 107–11, 114, 134; future 4, 107–8; insurance 112–13; investment 136; regulation 54, 100, 122–4, 135

Barnier, M. 8–9
barriers to trade: changes to 7, 34, 84; driving force 40, 48; history 26, 70; UN harmonization 54; vehicle standards 31
Bentley 24
Bloomberg, M. 120
BMW 19, 25–6, 31, 78, 94, 103
Brown, J. 119

California: loss of manufacturing 128, 131–2; regulatory processes 73, 119
carbon: emissions 66, 113; control of 69; footprint 78; investment 103
carbon dioxide (CO_2): measurement 75–6; production impact 135; regulation 3, 32, 39, 71, 74; targets 95; volume 66
carbon monoxide (CO) 37, 71
CARS 2020 54
Centered High Mounted Stop Light (CHMSL) 88–9

Chakrabarti, V. 124
Chevrolet 103
China: growth 12, 21; exports 13; UN Agreement participation 52; AV regulations 111
Citroen 1
Coase, R. 31, 67
Common Customs Tariff 33
congestion 2–4, 32, 69, 119–20, 137
contracting parties 46–52
Corporate Average Fuel Economy (CAFE) 73, 78

Defense Advanced Research Programs Agency (DARPA) 108
diesel 3, 32, 64–5, 103, 120
Directorate of Enterprise and Industry 40

electric vehicles (EV): counting towards targets 95; development 2–4, 69; disruption impact 99–107; investment 136; limitations 137; manufacturing impact 131, 138; regulatory changes 135; with autonomous vehicles 113–4, 124
Electronic Stability Control (ESC) 89–92
employees 17, 24, 106
employment 13–4, 17, 21–5, 100, 113, 129
Energy Policy and Conservation Act 73
Environmental Protection Agency (EPA) 66, 73, 77, 104–5, 135
Euro 1–6 standards 37, 39, 71

146 *Index*

European Commission 8, 36, 39–40, 54–5, 76, 134–5
European Economic Area 84–5
European Parliament 38–57
export(s): history 25–6; production impact 22; regulation 32–6, 49, 70; risk of loss 25, 135; size 8, 12–14, 18, 94
externalities 31, 68–9, 71, 87

Facilitated Customs Arrangement 7
Federal Automated Vehicles Policy 123
Federal Motor Vehicle Safety Standards (FMVSS) 86, 92, 135
Fiat 1, 25, 77
financial services 11, 21–2
Ford 16, 25, 31, 93, 102, 128
four freedoms 8, 26, 32
France: industry size 13–4; service sector 17; sales location 25, 31
free movement: development 70, 84; importance 7–9, 138; logistics impact 92; rules of origin 32–5; type-approval 37
free trade 7, 84, 87, 108, 130
free trade agreement (FTA) 33, 35–6

GEAR 2030 55–6
General Motors 26, 78, 107, 128, 131
Germany 13–4, 17, 25, 91, 106
Global Technical Regulations (GTR) 45–6, 48–52, 54
greenhouse gas 63, 66–7, 71, 73, 76, 135
Gross Domestic Product (GDP) 17–21, 120, 128–30
The Guardian 25

Hawes, M. 35–6
Holden 128, 131
homologation 85
Honda 16, 19, 26, 78
House of Commons: committees 25, 130
hydrocarbon 37, 71
Hyundai 13, 22, 103, 105

India 16, 21, 52
Industrial Reorganisation Corporation 15
Industrial Strategy 25, 103, 134
insurance 21, 89, 112, 113, 123
International Automotive Summit 25
International Organization of Motor Vehicle Manufacturers (OICA) 13–4

Jaguar 1, 16, 19, 24–6, 105
Japan: end of Australia assembly 130; industry development 15–6; production system 93; UN Agreement voting 51–2, 56;
just-in-time 22, 36, 93

Khan, S. 119, 121
Kia 103, 105

labour: losses from pollution 63; productivity 13–4, 22–3; restricted movement 25; requirements for 106, 129, 134
Lada 1
Land Rover 16, 19, 24–6
lean manufacturing 21
Leyland 29
local content 26, 36, 128–9
logistics 27, 85, 92–4, 128, 138
London: Automotive Summit 25; independent regulations 69, 118–9
Lotus 24

May, T. 55–6
Mercedes Benz 1, 90, 94, 106
Mini 24
Minford, P. 130
most favoured nation 33
My MPG 77

National Highway Traffic Safety Administration (NHTSA) 86, 88–9, 90–1, 110, 123, 135
National Rivers Authority 69
National Traffic and Motor Vehicle Safety Act 72
New European Driving Cycle (NEDC) 74, 76

Index 147

New Zealand: loss of vehicle manufacturing 22, 128–30, 136
Nissan 11, 16, 19, 26, 94, 103
nitrogen oxides (NOx) 63, 65, 71, 73, 76
Nordhaus, W. 69
normative issues 67, 87
Notification of Withdrawal 2, 6

Obama administration 73, 78
Office for National Statistics 17, 24
Organization of the Petroleum Exporting Countries (OPEC) 73
original equipment manufacturers (OEM) 93

Paris: independent regulations 69, 119
particulate matter ($PM_{2.5}$) 32, 63–5, 68, 71
petrol 32, 37, 67, 71–3, 101–4
Peugeot 25
pollution: electric vehicles 113; from vehicles 30–2; impact 62–3, 65–8; regulation development 70, 73, 95, 120; UN regulations 45–6, 54
Portable Emission Measuring Systems (PEMS) 76–7
price of entry 3–4, 8
productivity 7, 16, 21–3, 67, 105
property rights 68, 87

Real Driving Emissions (RDE) 39, 76
referendum 1, 6, 92, 119
Renault 25
Rolls-Royce 24
Rover 16, 19, 24–6, 106
rules of origin 30–6

Seoul: independent regulations 119
services: employment 17; financial 11; free movement 7–9, 26, 84, 136; productivity 21
Single European Act (SEA) 71
Smart 103
Society of Automotive Engineers (SAE) 72, 110
Society of Motor Manufacturers & Traders (SMMT) 25
South Africa 22

South Korea 13, 21–2
Spain 13, 14
supply chain 2, 15, 31, 35, 136

targets 3, 71, 95, 111
tariff: cost 8, 25, 36, 94, 138; ending protection 128–30; history 26; market access 84–5; regain control 7, 34; rules of origin 31, 33, 35
Tata 16
technology: automated vehicles 110–11, 113, 136–7, batteries 104; industry 35; production requirements 22; regulation 88–92;
Tesla 103–4, 131
testing procedures 22, 77, 135
Toyoda, K. 93
Toyota 15, 26, 92–4, 128
Toyota Production System (TPS) 93
Trabant 1
Treaty of Rome 70
Treaty on the Functioning of the European Union (TFEU) 33–4
Triumph 24
Trump administration 73, 77–8, 123
type-approval 36–9, 40–1, 44, 55, 74

UK Department for Transport 66
UN 1958 Agreement 38, 46–51, 53–6
UN 1997 Agreement 46–7, 49
UN 1998 Agreement 46, 48–9, 51–3, 55–6
UN Economic and Social Committee (ECOSOC) 45, 48, 52–4
UN Economic Commission for Europe (UNECE) 36–40, 44–7, 49–50, 53–7, 70–1, 114
UN Regulations 45, 47–51, 53–5

Vauxhall 19, 25, 94
Volkswagen (VW): sales concentration 25; emissions testing scandal 62, 77, 79, 122

White Paper 6–9, 73, 100, 135
Whole Vehicle Type Approval System (WVTA) 36–7, 40, 44, 55
Working Group on Motor Vehicles (E01295) 39

148 *Index*

Working Party on the Construction of Vehicles 40, 70
World Forum for Harmonization of Vehicle Regulations (WP.29) 45–6, 48, 52, 54, 56, 135

World Health Organisation (WHO) 63–4
'World-Harmonized Light-duty Vehicle Test Procedure' (WLTP) 39, 76